To♡: Charlyne

MW00712385

Wish you
Happy birthday
!!!

Charlotte Ong your
Cousin

29 July

BOOKS IN
THIS SERIES

THE DIARY OF AMOS LEE

Girls, Guts and Glory!

Written by
ADELINE FOO

Illustrated by
STEPHANIE WONG

E

EPIGRAM BOOKS / SINGAPORE

Copyright © 2009 by Adeline Foo
All rights reserved.

Published in Singapore by Epigram Books
www.epigrambooks.sg

Cover design by Stephanie Wong
Illustrations © 2009 by Stephanie Wong

NATIONAL LIBRARY BOARD SINGAPORE
CATALOGUING IN PUBLICATION DATA
Foo, Adeline, 1971–
The diary of Amos Lee: I sit, I write, I flush! / written by Adeline Foo,
illustrated by Stephanie Wong. – 2nd ed. – Singapore: Epigram, 2012.
p. cm.
ISBN: 978-981-07-2678-2 (pbk.)

1. Boys – Singapore – Diaries – Juvenile fiction.
2. Children – Singapore – Diaries – Juvenile fiction.
3. Singapore – Juvenile fiction. I. Wong, Stephanie, 1979– II. Title.

PZ7
S823 -- dc23 OCN794961501

This is a work of fiction. Names, characters, places, and incidents
either are the product of the author's imagination or are
used fictitiously. Any resemblance to actual persons,
living or dead, events, or locales is entirely coincidental.

Second Edition
10 9 8 7 6 5 4 3 2 1

Last year I became famous for the wrong reason. I was known as the first boy in the whole world to write his diary in the toilet!

I still write from the toilet this year. It's the only place I can go to get away from my troubles - like Michael, the ex-prefect bully, who is in the school swimming team with me. I think he's secretly training to be a dolphin! There's also our crazy Coach, a former army man who drives us nuts in training. Plus I fell out with my best friend, Alvin, over a girl, of all things! And to top it all off, my sister got possessed by a weird curse, and started building monster dolls to fight my baby brother's arrival!

I take my diary wherever I go as I know there are those who want to get their hands on it. For I know secrets, like breaking my sister's curse and how babies are made. This diary really beats what you can find on the internet, about re-pro-dark-sion and stuff.

Reproduction! Really, I didn't know that interested you, Amos. And please use the dictionary!

Mum, the Toilet English Teacher.
Some things never change.

MY MUM

Women are really strange when they are pregnant. They eat lots of weird stuff in the middle of the night, put on weight, then whine about being fat. I caught Mum doing weight lifts in the kitchen, with a watermelon! She said she needed to work off extra calories from eating too much.

MY SISTER

She's suffering from anxiety. I caught her disfiguring potatoes in the kitchen. She was making ugly faces on them with a fork, muttering under her breath, "I hate you, I hate you!" Still as Whiny, Pesky and Irritating as ever. That's WPI, for short.

MY DAD

He's so proud that Mum is pregnant. A baby bonus, he keeps saying. Something about the government giving us money for having a third child. I caught him putting his cheek to Mum's stomach, crooning, "Yoohoo... can you hear Papa? My babeee boh-nussss..."

Sometimes I wonder if I am the only normal person in this family. Something tells me that this diary is no longer safe in the toilet. I must not leave it where crazy people <u>can read</u> it and vent their ~~flush-tra-tion~~ in it.

Frustration! And really, you should use the dictionary!

A frustrated and neurotic mum. I must find a secret hiding place where she cannot find my diary.

POOR ME, A SLAVE TO HOUSEWORK

I don't like Mum's gai-ni-colon-gist very much. He ordered complete bed rest for Mum, to "preserve the state of baby." No cooking or housework allowed! Dad said with gadgets like the washing machine and vacuum cleaner, any child can help around the house, so I have just been made the Official Laundry Boy and Vacuum Cleaner Operator of the Lee Family! And Dad said he would NOT be paying me for my labour. This is a serious act of child abuse!

Amos, you're expected to help for free. And I believe the correct term is obstetrician, not gynaecologist!

How did she find my diary? I hid it under my bed!

Sunday, 4 January

I put up an ad at our flat's lift landing. "Help Wanted For Housework!" WPI saw it and I hired her on the spot. I told her it would be easy - all she has to do is vacuum the house when Mum is out and do the laundry when Mum is taking her nap. I will pay her five potato chips for every job done.

Dad was right - any child can do housework!

BACK TO SCHOOL!

There is a new kid in school. Her
name is Somaly. She's a foreign
student from Cambodia. Humph!
Alvin was soooooooooooo keen
to find out more about her and kept asking me what
I thought of her. Not much, really. Why should I care
about some girl?

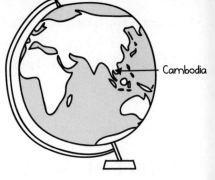

Cambodia

4pm

It's great to be back at school! I miss hanging out with
my best friends, Alvin and Anthony. Alvin said he got a new
pet over the holidays. Hmm... wonder what it is this time?
Last year his dad bought him frogs!

Anthony said he spent his entire holidays mugging.
His mum made him go for tuition four times a week,
and attend five study camps for English, Mandarin,
Mathematics and Science. I asked him what the fifth
camp was for and he said sheepishly, "How to Score in
Exams." That's his punishment for being last in class last
year. Poor Anthony.

Thursday, 8 January

ALVIN'S NEW PET

Alvin brought his pet to school today.
It's a spider! And for some unknown
reason, he was dying to show it

7

to Somaly. I was so irritated with him. Instead of paying attention in class, he kept turning back to look at her. What is wrong with him?

Friday, 9 January

SOMETHING FISHY IS GOING ON

Alvin disappeared during recess. I couldn't find him anywhere! Anthony said he saw Alvin with Somaly, in the school garden shed. What were they doing together?

Monday, 12 January

A CRISIS!

Alvin lost his spider in school today! He was really upset. I can't believe how careless he was. I got everyone in class to help look for it, but it seemed ridiculous. How were we supposed to recognise it? Anthony even offered to put up posters of the missing spider in all the toilets. I thought that was a silly idea but didn't say anything. How could anyone possibly find it?

Tuesday, 13 January

SPIDER FOUND!

We spent the entire afternoon after school looking for Alvin's silly spider! In the classroom and the garden shed.

We even combed the ceilings with torchlights. Imagine how irritated I felt when it was Somaly who found the spider. She saw something moving on Anthony's head and true enough, it was the spider. It must have fallen on his head, scared by a bright torchlight. Alvin was so happy that he hugged Somaly! Hugged her! Yeeks, he was trying to get close to her. Worse still, he didn't even thank Anthony or I.

I asked Alvin how sure he was that the spider Somaly found was his spider. He said, "I recognise the way it strokes its legs." Great, my best friend thinks he is some kind of <u>spider scientist</u>.

The word is arachnologist, Amos. Alvin is just being kind to Somaly, since she's so far from home. And you are supposed to help around the house, not pay your sister potato chips to do it for you!

My goodness! I had been hiding this behind the cupboard. How did Mum find it? Nothing escapes her.

Friday, 16 January

SOMALY THE SPIDER QUEEN

Yup, the new kid in school has sucked my best friend into her web of deceit. Alvin will do anything for his Spider

Queen. Today, I saw them in the library! Alvin, of all people! Since when did he get so studious? But I saw what he was reading. It was The Adventures of Peter Parker. What a joke. He's just pretending to be a good boy, to get close to Somaly.

3pm

Anthony called me. He said he saw Alvin and Somaly with TWO spiders today. Where did the second one come from? Oh man!

8pm

I called Alvin to ask about the second spider.
He explained that it was a present for Somaly. He found out that she used to catch spiders back in Cambodia to play with. He even told me that they are trying to mate their spiders and make spider babies. I'm going to puke after this.

Thursday, 22 January

ALVIN'S NEW INTEREST

Alvin just called. He said he had borrowed the book Charlotte's Web from the library today. It was Somaly who had told him it was a good book. At first, I couldn't believe Alvin was being so obedient, reading what Somaly likes. But, while we were talking, he confessed that he had borrowed the DVD of the movie Charlotte's Web, not the book. He said it was faster to watch the movie than read the book. So, Alvin has not changed after all!

Wednesday, 28 January
_____

SHOW & TELL

Alvin talked about Charlotte's Web during Show & Tell. He did such a good job of dissecting the story and talking about the characters that Teacher ordered all of us to read the book! Oh man... I could see Somaly gazing at him with stars in her eyes. Only I know how he knew so much. I'm going to borrow the DVD from him, and if he doesn't want to lend it to me, I will tell his "girlfriend" the truth.

Saturday, 31 January
_____

ABOUT SPIDERS AND PIGS

I watched Charlotte's Web with WPI this afternoon. During dinner, she refused to eat the sausages Mum cooked. She even accused Mum of murdering Wilbur, the pig in the story. Really, so dramatic! The silly girl ate plain rice for dinner, as Mum had only cooked fried sausages, eggs and vegetables. WPI said she did not want to be guilty of eating unborn chicks as well.

After finishing my homework, I googled to find out more about spiders. They are really amazing creatures. I called Anthony to tell him what I found out, but he didn't want to hear any of it. He said he had been having nightmares about the spider that was found on his head. He even asked me if he should shave himself bald!

I called Alvin next but I didn't get to say very much. He went on and on about how Somaly was like Charlotte, the spider. He called her a misunderstood creature. Really, who cares about Somaly? I think Alvin is Somaly's only friend in class. The other kids in school are not really mixing with her.

Sunday, 1 February

WPI AND HER SPIDERS

I shouldn't have asked WPI to watch the movie with me. Last night, she had a bad dream. She screamed so loudly that Dad and Mum rushed into our bedroom. She said she saw black spider monsters on the wall. My sister has such an incredible imagination. Mum broke down crying, saying it was a bad omen to see black spiders in the house. What is it with these women?

2pm

I can't believe I got grounded for educating my sister! No computer for a week. Mum said it was all my fault, for corrupting her mind with a spider movie. Hey, strong words here, Mum! I know you are suffering from (ho-moan-nal) imbalance – that's what Dad said – but don't blame me if your daughter can see visions on the wall! I think this is all Alvin's fault. He's the one who got all of us started on spiders in the first place!

It's hormonal!
I am perfectly normal!

No mad person will admit that they are crazy. My mum must be suffering from a nervous breakdown and my sister is loony. I should not have left my diary in my school bag. I must be more careful next time.

FIELD TRIP

We visited the Reflections at Bukit Chandu today, a World War Two In-ter-pre-ta-tive Centre. It's Total Defence Day this Sunday – TD Day is the day we remember Singapore falling to the Japanese during World War Two. Felt good to get out of class!

We had a good time running around the place, scaring ourselves by making ghostly noises. I wouldn't want to be locked up at Bukit Chandu overnight. It was the place where the last regiment of Malay soldiers was killed while defending Singapore against the advancing Japanese army. Oooooooh.......!

Anthony called. He said he saw Alvin giving Somaly an envelope at Bukit Chandu. I wonder what was in it.

Monday, 16 February

ALVIN'S ENVELOPE

I asked Alvin what he gave Somaly at Bukit Chandu. He grinned and said it was a Valentine's Day card. I couldn't believe my ears! When I asked him if he really liked her, he replied that they were just good friends. The Valentine's Day card was to celebrate their baby spiders being born. He looked like a proud father as he went on and on about his cute little "babies". Wow, imagine that. First, two spiders, then now, we have a freaking spider army running around in school. I must tell Anthony that his head will be under siege next!

Friday, 20 February

WHAT I WANT TO BE WHEN I GROW UP

The new relief teacher was not happy with my composition. I wrote about my ambition to be a New Age Spiderman in the 21st Century, and she wrote in my exercise book, "Is this for real?" Why can't I dream about what I would like to be when I grow up?

Dad wanted to be like Carl Lewis, the world's fastest runner during his time. As a student, he was inspired to train and compete in inter-school competitions, and he even won a few trophies! Mum wanted to be a vet when she was young, but she never became one as she tended to faint at the sight of blood. But she continued loving animals and brought sick, stray kittens home to nurse before she got married. She never became a vet, but she still loves animals and writes about them sometimes in her job as a magazine writer.

So why can't I be a New Age Spiderman? Science is so advanced, I'm sure someone will invent a sticky glue that will allow us to climb buildings without aid. In fact, there is a stunt man who calls himself the Incredible Human Spider and he scales tall buildings for a living. I saw him on TV last year. Imagine getting paid for such loony feats! What's wrong with wanting to be a New Age Spiderman?

Friday, 27 February

PARENT-TEACHER CONFERENCE

Dad and Mum were called up to see my teacher. I hid outside the classroom to listen to what they were talking about. I heard words like "disturbed", "insecurity" and "a lunatic." Why are they talking about WPI?

8pm

FATHER AND SON TALK

Dad had a good chat with me tonight. He asked if I was having problems at school. I told him I was upset that Alvin had abandoned me for his new girlfriend. Anthony isn't exactly fun to hang around with. The 3As are just not the same without Alvin. Dad also asked if I was anxious about

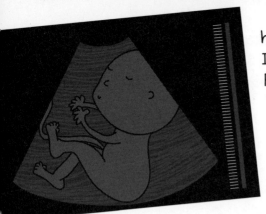

having a baby brother. Is he kidding? I am so RELIEVED this family will have more of the male species. It is really good news.

After our chat, I told WPI that Baby is going to be a boy. I thought she took the news quite well. I know she has always wanted a baby sister, but well, too bad. You don't always get what you wish for.

Sunday, 1 March

WPI IS ACTING WEIRD

WPI is acting really weird. I caught her rinsing her paint palette when doing the laundry. I peeped inside the washing machine and saw filthy blue clothes. They were the new clothes for Baby! I was so horrified. How could she do this!

Mum's going to kill me! I can't even trust my hired help now! I spent two hours rinsing all of Baby's clothes in clean water. When I went into the bedroom, I caught WPI doodling on Baby's crib sheets! She said it was an accident but I don't believe her. Last night, I thought I heard her chanting in her sleep. When I woke her up, she mumbled that she was

going to stuff Baby into a pillowcase! This is no good. Who can I confide in? I seriously think my sister is a disturbed, insecure lunatic. Even my teacher said it, right?

CONFIDING IN ALVIN

I caught Alvin before classes started. I told him about WPI seeing black spider monsters on the wall and acting weird. When he said he believed me, I felt so happy! Alvin told me he would seek Somaly's help. He said that she may know about voodoo chants and how to unlock a curse. It's great that I'm going to get help for my sister.

SOMALY'S VOODOO CHANT

I stumbled on Somaly doing a voodoo chant with a group of girls in a corner of school. She did circles in the air with her elbow, and chanted, "We must, we must, we must increase our bust!" Huh? What bust? Maybe Somaly is seeking voodoo aid to bust my sister's curse. Alvin must have spoken to her. I sneaked away before the girls saw me.

WPI AND HER MONSTER DOLLS

It's getting worse. WPI must be possessed! She is
building ugly, monster dolls in her bedroom secretly.
I saw her taking apart all her dolls' body parts, and
re-attaching them, wrong heads to wrong body parts.
They looked hideous!

11pm

I recited Somaly's voodoo
chant over WPI as she
was sleeping.

"I bust, I bust, I bust your
curse TO-NIGHT!" I thought
it worked when WPI stirred
in her sleep. But she woke
up screaming, yelling to Mum
that I was strangling her! Mum was so
mad, she told me to get out of the room. I am sleeping
on the sofa tonight. Sheesh...

THE VOODOO CHANT

I caught Alvin with Somaly today and told him I used
the chant on WPI. He looked confused and asked me
to demonstrate what I did. I chanted, "I bust, I bust,
I bust your curse TO-NIGHT!" I even repeated the elbow-
circling act. Somaly suddenly looked really red in the face.

I thought I got it wrong, so I repeated the chant, and that was when I realised what the girls were chanting about! Oh man... how silly of me. They were hoping to expand their bust, for big boobs. How disgusting! I thought it was silly, then I laughed at Somaly! That was when Alvin shoved me and I got really mad.

THIS IS IT! He shoved me because of a girl. He is no longer my best friend. He has crossed over to the dark side.

Tuesday, 10 March

MICHAEL

I bumped into Michael this morning. Anthony said he heard that Michael's parents transferred him to another school nearer his home, to save money from putting him on the school bus. But then, the principal offered to pick Michael up from his flat in the mornings. So he's back at our school.

Funny, we haven't seen him since the start of school, and then suddenly he pops up! Michael looks bigger and meaner, but at least I think he will leave me alone now. He used to pick on me a great deal, until I helped to raise funds for his operation when he got into an accident last year. I hope he remembers he owes me a big favour!

POOL INCIDENT

Today is the start of a new sports programme in our school - mass swimming for everyone. A new coach has been brought in to help us. I knew he was a bit psycho when he shouted at us, "Fall in!" Anthony said he heard that the coach used to be from the army. That explains why he barks out orders in a booming voice and made all of us do 100 half-squats for warm-up!

Michael stood in front of me. He got so energised that I heard his swimming trunks rip. I started giggling and when everyone turned to look at me, I yelled out, "Watch out, we can see your backside!" He glared at me, covered his bum and ran to the toilet. We didn't see him after that. Must have gone straight home.

Wednesday, 18 March

ACCIDENT AT THE POOL

What a horrible day. I saw Michael at the pool. It was my turn to swim and he shoved me from behind. When I surfaced, he just laughed and said it was for fun. I wasn't sure if he was telling the truth, but the worst part was when I thought I saw Alvin laughing too. How could he! I felt so hurt. Alvin has really crossed over to the dark side. Michael came up to me to apologise after that. But I don't think he was sincere. Alvin did not even come over to see if I was okay. I saw him walking off with Somaly. They were holding a box and giggling together. Sheesh... I wonder what they are up to?

Friday, 20 March

COMPETITIVE SWIMMING

Coach told us he will be conducting competitive swimming classes two times a week. For me, I will be swimming three times a week, as I have chosen swimming as my co-curricular activity (CCA). So have Anthony, Alvin and Michael. I was irritated to discover that Somaly has also

signed up for swimming as her CCA. Looks like we're going to see a great deal of one another this year. Anyway, I'm really excited about this new programme. I like swimming because everyone is equal in the water, regardless of size. And it doesn't take much effort to swim. Coach, however, is a bit scary. During practice today, he was shouting out marching orders as we swam, "Move it! Move it! Left, right, left, right, move your arms and legs! Left, right, left, right!" He's craaaaazy!

Anthony complained that Coach was driving him nuts and he can't swim properly with someone yelling at him all the time. He said it reminds him too much of his mum! I just ignored the yelling. At the end of practice, Coach did a swimming selection for the school team, and I made it! I swam 100m in under two minutes. Anthony and Alvin got through too, but they were slower than me! Michael also got in - he did 100m in just over two minutes. Well, he may be bigger, but I'm faster. So there!

9am

It is the start of the school holidays, but Mum said she is too tired to bring WPI and I out to our usual haunts – the library and the bookstores. In any case, Coach has asked the swimming team to practise during the holidays, so I will be quite busy!

6pm

Michael is back to his old self. He laughed at me at the pool this afternoon, saying that he can beat me at swimming any time. He even pointed at my private part and called me Small Willy! I HATE HIM! Why is he picking on me? Well, I got back at him immediately by coming in first during today's 100m freestyle practice. So there!

The girls' team also did the 100m freestyle. I didn't realise that Somaly had also made it to the swimming team – she swam, and clocked a faster timing than Michael! I was so happy that she beat Michael that for once, I felt like hugging her! But of course, I restrained myself. Michael was really red in the face – beaten by a girl! It's nice to see a girl beating him. So long as she remains behind me.

A WASTED DAY

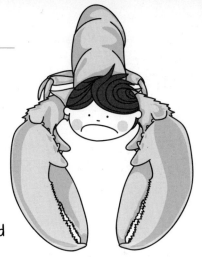

Someone cut up my swimming trunks! As I was about to put them on in the locker room, I noticed the tear. I was furious! I spent the afternoon watching everyone else swim while I baked in the sun. It was so hot that when practice ended, Michael walked over and said, "Look at you, a red lobster with a small willy!" I felt like pushing him into the pool. When I told Anthony about my swimming trunks, he whispered that he had seen Michael taking out a pair of scissors in the locker room. It must be him! He probably hoped my trunks would tear after I had put them on. Lucky thing I noticed it before my bum got exposed. I am going to get you, Michael!

Thursday, 26 March

LIZARD IN THE HOUSE!

Po-Po visited us today. It is great having Po-Po back in Singapore. We haven't seen her since Christmas last year, when Ah Kong and her went to stay with relatives in China. I overheard Mum talking to Po-Po about the lizards in our house. She was complaining that we have one crazy lizard that has been feeding off discarded rice in the kitchen sink. Whatever happened to old-fashioned house lizards that eat mosquitoes?

Mum told Po-Po she is terrified of the lizard in the sink, so I offered to catch it for her. I bought a lizard trap and laid some rice on it.

11pm

I went to check my lizard trap. The lizard didn't get stuck, but it left its tail behind. It was gross. I stuck some bread on a new trap. I hope this works!

Friday, 27 March

9am

Got it! The lizard was stuck on the trap. It's the same one alright because it was missing a tail. Hmm...

7pm

This afternoon, I left a gift for Michael. I stuck it in his bag in the locker room. It was so satisfying when I heard him scream after practice. He put his hand into his bag and pulled out my lizard trap. I don't know which was funnier, seeing the lizard staring at him, minus a tail, or seeing Michael's terrified face.

Everyone roared with laughter! Michael was swearing when he ran out of the locker room. Revenge is sweet.

Amos, I have said many times you are supposed to walk away from bullies, not get back at them!

How did she find my diary? I have been hiding this for the last month in Mum's skinny jeans!

I was checking my jeans to see how fat I've grown, Amos.

Right, I cannot hide the diary in the same place for too long. Lesson learnt!

Monday, 30 March

HURRAY! ANTHONY MADE PREFECT

Today is our first day back at school after the holidays. It was a nice surprise when Teacher announced that Anthony will be made prefect this year! I feel so happy for him! He may be last in class, but the principal said Anthony has talents not many people have – his computer skills. He is a whiz kid, very good with online research and knows all about computers and e-games! Anthony was also very happy. He said, "I think my mum will be pleased."

Michael must be feeling sore that he wasn't made prefect this year. Serves him right! Hmm... my buddy is now a prefect. Guess it will be useful to have a friend in high places.

PHYSICAL EXAMINATION IN SCHOOL

11am

Nurses visited the school today. We had our eyes checked, and our height and body fat taken. My Body Mass Index was above the limit for my height. I didn't get to see what was written in my report, but I saw the nurse pass a list of names to Teacher.

3pm

Someone took the names of all the fat kids from Teacher and wrote on the whiteboard today - "OBESE, Desperate Weight Loss Needed!" Imagine my horror when I saw my name on the board, with three other names of my classmates. I am now officially a FAT kid.

Wednesday, 1 April

SLIM CLUB

Coach recruited all the FAT kids into a special club. He called it the Slim Club, a brisk walking and jogging club for FAT kids. Really, is this some kind of April Fool's Day joke? Don't they realise that they are hurting our self-esteem?

Even calling it a Slim Club doesn't help. Anyone can tell it's a bunch of FAT kids trying to lose weight when we are seen walking and jogging together! How totally em-bear-ass-ing! To top it all off, Coach made us shout out a ridiculous chant as we "jogged" around the school field:

"I don't know but I've been told!
Slim Club kids are on the roll!
I don't know but it's been said!
Slim Club kids are fighting fit!"

Where can I hide my face now? I heard Coach saying to another teacher that it's called reverse sai-co-logy. Is that what they teach you in the army? How to play mind games?

It's embarrassing and psychology! You're not fat, Amos. You just have heavy bones. It runs in the family. But maybe you should stop eating all those fried chicken wings!

Aw... thanks Mum! Hey, how did you manage to find my diary this time? I put it behind all the lizard traps in the cupboard!

BACK TO SPIDERS

I finally found out what Alvin and Somaly are up to at the swimming pool. I have been noticing them carrying a box around and they are always giggling together! Today, I managed to peek at the box while they weren't looking. They have been bringing their spiders to the pool! I even saw them conducting all these silly experiments, like putting their "babies" in a tub of water to see them swim!

Ugh. I must report them to the principal! Or maybe someone else can be persuaded to do the job...

NO MORE SPIDERS!

Anthony reported to Coach that Alvin and Somaly were playing with spiders at the swimming pool. Coach was horrified. He went up to them and barked, "No spiders shall invade my territory!" He then ordered both of them to release all their spiders in the field behind the pool. Anthony said he secretly followed Alvin and Somaly to the field and after seeing all those baby spiders being released, he thought he was going to have a nightmare. I thought he felt guilty, about squealing on them. But no, he said he just felt sick, thinking about an army of spiders invading his head.

I'm glad I got Anthony to report this to Coach. Alvin and Somaly are going too far by bringing spiders to the swimming pool.

Tuesday, 14 April

FAMOUS QUOTES

I got hauled up in class, AGAIN! We were asked to list four famous quotes by important people or historic figures. These must be sayings that most people in the world can recognise. How difficult can that be? I was so diligent, I even added a fifth quote.

FAMOUS QUOTES SUBMITTED BY AMOS LEE

1 Enough! Enough is enough.

2 Stop it right now or you're going to get it.

3 You'd better watch it. You're going to get it when we get home.

4 Stop crying or I'll give you something real to cry about.

5 Shut up and sit down!

Who wouldn't recognise any of these famous quotes? A mother is a very important person, isn't she? Anyone in the world can recognise these sayings, even if they are said in different languages. Teacher said I am too smart for my own good. He's just jealous I can think for myself.

It's, *"Silence! And please stop jumping up and down!"*

Isn't that what I said? "SHUT UP AND SIT DOWN!" Sheesh... she can even find my diary when I hide them with the encyclopedias. Amazing.

Wednesday, 15 April

MOUNT EVEREST

Mum has been following the reports of a Singapore women's team climbing Mount Everest. I wonder why she's so interested. It's just a mountain expedition and men have been climbing mountains since prehistoric times.

Today, Mum proudly exclaimed that the Singapore Women's Everest Expedition has made it to the base camp at the foot of Mount Everest. Can they make it to the top?

FALSE ALARM

Mum thought Baby was early. She had bad cramps last night! Dad drove her to the hospital. They were there for two hours, but the contractions stopped. Mum came home this morning. It was a false alarm. Baby is being really cheeky, scaring everyone like this.

Poor Mum, she looks exhausted from all the excitement.

KARATE KID

Every night at 10pm, Baby would start stirring and kicking and Mum would ask me to feel her stomach. Wow, a karate kid in the making! Last night she allowed me to shine a torchlight at her stomach, and Baby kicked in response! He can see the light!

WPI is not really keen to join in with all these experiments. She just sulks and plays with her dolls. She's such a spoilsport. Just jealous that Baby is getting all the attention, even before he's born. It's time she faces the fact that she is no longer the baby of the family.

SPIDER BABY

3pm

Alvin and Somaly came up to me during recess and said they had a present for me.

Imagine my surprise when they gave me a cute baby spider in a matchbox! Alvin said, "We managed to save a few before we released the rest into the wild!" I thought I saw tears in his eyes – he's so dramatic. Somaly said, "Alvin would like to give you a spider and be friends again. Right, Alvin?" She nudged him very hard and he nodded silently.

Oh man... I feel so guilty. They had no clue I was the one who persuaded Anthony to report them to Coach. I kept quiet and took the baby spider home.

8pm

I spent the entire afternoon looking at the baby spider under a magnifying glass. It's quite interesting. No wonder Alvin and Somaly are so fascinated with their spiders! I wonder how spiders make babies. The movie Charlotte's Web didn't show any of that. But Charlotte's egg sac carried lots of baby spiders, and they were quite cute.

10pm

Found LOTS of information on making babies on the internet!

BABY TALK

Mum just asked if I was curious how babies are made.
I knew it! She must have read my diary, AGAIN! But she
didn't write anything in it this time. Anyway, I just ignored
her question and asked her to tell me more about the
women's team climbing Mount Everest. She totally forgot
about everything and went on and on about how long the
team has been training for, how cold the weather is and
how much stamina it must have taken them to reach
base camp. Ha ha, managed to trick her!

MUM'S BIG BOOK OF MAKING BABIES

When I came home from
swimming practice today,
Mum passed me a book called
Conception, Pregnancy and
Birth by Dr Miriam Stoppard to
read. The pictures in the book
are so graphic!

This book is written by a doctor. After looking through it,
I now understand how babies are made. How exciting – I'm
now an expert on making babies, both spider and human
ones! Maybe second only to Dr Miriam Stoppard. Really, this
is very interesting science! Wait till I tell Anthony about
what I've learned from Dr Stoppard!

ANTHONY'S GOOD IDEA

Anthony was cool when I said I knew how babies were made. He said he already knew. Somehow, I'm not surprised. Then, he said something really exciting! He wanted us to do a science magazine together. I could write two features on how baby spiders and human babies are made, and Anthony would look for really good drawings on the internet. Boy, are we clever!

Anthony said we could sell copies of our magazine and make lots of money. Yeah! This beats having to earn money selling things

or dressing up as a clown at birthday parties. That was what I did to save up to buy a PlayStation Portable last year. Anthony asked what happened to the Project PSP money. The money is safe in the bank, but since almost everyone in class has a PSP now, I don't need to buy one anymore. I just have to borrow one to play!

But I told him I would like to buy a handphone. Mum thinks I'm too young to own one, but I think it would be useful to have, to send SMSes or to play games. But first, let's get on with this magazine. Mum can help with editing it, since she has quit her writing job.

OUR SCIENCE MAGAZINE

Anthony used Microsoft Office Publisher on his computer to design our magazine. It was so easy to do – we had hundreds of templates to choose from! We had a hard time thinking of a catchy name. Finally, we decided on "The Amos & Anthony Science Observer", A^{2}SO for short.

ISSUE #1 | **A^{2}SO** | **The Amos & Anthony Science Observer**

SPIDER MATES
BY AMOS LEE

In the book Charlotte's Web by E.B. White, we read about how Charlotte laid many babies before she died at the end of the story. The idea of having her live on through her children touched me. I was drawn by the selfless act of a mother giving birth to her babies. This issue explains how spiders mate.

In understanding how spiders mate, we have to look at the concept of a lock and key. The male spider's male organ, called a palp, represents the key that seeks the lock, a female spider's epigyne. As with keys and locks, the wrong key will not open the lock. What this means is that for successful mating, spiders must find the right mate from the same species.

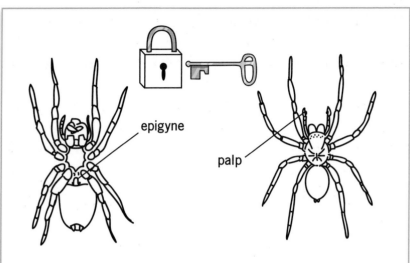

epigyne

palp

Before mating, a female spider gives off a scent that attracts a male spider. The male spider goes into a courtship dance, where it taps and strokes its legs. When the female spider is ready to receive him, she will open her fangs, which the male spider will catch and hold, while he proceeds to copulate, drumming his palp on her epigyne. The transfer of sperm from male palp to female epigyne takes place and this leads to the fertilisation of eggs, in the making of spider babies. Different species of spiders mate differently. Some spiders mount the backs of their female counterparts, and then lean in from behind to insert their palp into the female spider's epigyne.

I showed Mum my article. She didn't freak out. She said I wrote it very well.

See, I figured that if I show her what I am up to, she won't need to go around looking for it. She has such a big belly, it's hard to bend and peep under the bed or look behind cupboards.

Mum said she loved the idea of a using a "lock and key" to describe mating and finding the "right key to fit a lock" in making babies. She said it's like a mature woman, meeting the right life partner and getting married before having children! OK, whatever. Anyway, Mum also suggested that I add information on how spiderlings are hatched. So cute, I like the term!

FROM EGG TO SPIDERLING
BY AMOS LEE

After the successful fertilisation of eggs, the female spider weaves a disc of silk to deposit her eggs. She will then spin more silk to envelope the newly-laid eggs to form an egg-sac. The spider will guard the egg-sac carrying it on its back. Some species have mothers that attach their egg-sacs to branches in trees or holes in tree bark, while waiting for the spiderlings to hatch.

Baby spiders look exactly like their parents when they are hatched (like in the movie Charlotte's Web). The newly-hatched spiderling feeds on the yolk it still holds in its body. After its first moulting (shedding), it will grow hair, claws and colour, and it will also be able to spin its own silk, to trap prey in its web for food.

Mum said she's very proud of my article. However she said that I would have to let the baby spider go as she did not want any spiders in our house. I released my spider "into the wild" this evening – downstairs in the grass patch near our void deck. I was sad to let him go, but I'm glad that I found out so much about making babies!

FROM EMBRYO TO BABY
BY AMOS LEE

HOW BABIES ARE CONCEIVED
– From The Big Book of Secrets!

A sperm from Dad meets an egg from Mum to form a cell with its own unique genetic qualities. This newly-created cell will divide and re-divide, until a baby, a new human being, is formed.

The baby's genetic qualities are inherited from both Dad and Mum, which explains why children born from the same parents have the same features or they may develop mannerisms or traits, similar to their parents as they grow. Some scientists have also proven that talents or inherent gifts are passed from parent to child.

HOW DOES A SPERM MEET AN EGG?

It happens when sperm is ejaculated from the male organ and enters a woman's reproductive tract to meet a mature egg. Fertilisation occurs when the sperm penetrates the ovum. The fertilised egg, which is called a zygote, divides itself repeatedly to become a ball of cells called a blastocyst. The blastocyst will attach itself to the wall of the woman's uterus and develop into an embryo and later a foetus, nine weeks after conception. It takes between 38 to 40 weeks for full growth before Baby is born.

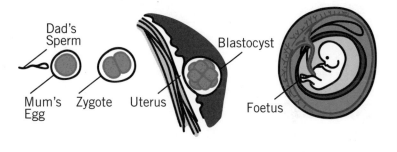

I did the drawings based on pictures Anthony found on the internet. Anthony said this will sell like hot cakes! Tomorrow we will bring this master copy to school and make at least 100 copies to sell.

Monday, 27 April

The first issue of A²SO sold out! We sold all 100 copies within 15 minutes of recess. Amazing. Alvin and Somaly came over and helped us distribute the copies and collect the money.

SECOND PRINT RUN FOR A²SO

We had to print another 100 copies. So many of our school mates wanted to read the A²SO. That's 200 copies sold within half an hour! Alvin said that if we were going to sell any more copies, he would do up a big poster and carry it around school, like a walking advertisement, to get us more publicity! I thought that was really nice of him.

Anthony asked if we could include Alvin and Somaly in our activities. I said Alvin is ok, but maybe we can leave Somaly out.

Thursday, 30 April

COMPLAINTS

Some girls complained to the principal about me promoting sex in school. Really, I thought we were just educating uninformed kids about sex. I had to make a copy of the A²SO and give it to the principal. Oh man... I'm going to get expelled!

Monday, 4 May

MORE TROUBLE!

2pm

Oh man... I'm beginning to regret doing the A²SO. Someone planted a box of lizard's eggs in my bag! I was initially deceived by the NERDS candy packaging. I did wonder why the sweets were all white. But I didn't suspect they had been tampered with! I was squishing the soft, gooey disgusting mess of "sweets" with my fingers, not realizing what they really were. My Science teacher happened to walk past, and she squealed at me before I could pop a couple into my mouth. "Stop, those are LIZARD'S EGGS!" she yelled. It was VILE and NAUSEATING just thinking about my close shave. Just whose dumb idea of a prank was it?

6pm

AN EXPERIMENT

Alvin and Anthony came over to my house to check out the lizard's eggs. We shut ourselves in the toilet and took them out of the box. They looked strange, like nano-sized eggs. Only spongier. No one would have guessed these were lizard's eggs. I would have preferred receiving a box of spider's eggs, but really, which kid would have the guts to comb ceilings to get them for a prank!

We had a good time laughing and clowning around with the eggs. We even challenged one another to pop one and hold it on the tongue. Alvin was awesome! He managed to hold one for exactly 20 seconds! Anthony managed six seconds before he started retching into the toilet bowl. And that was when WPI walked in on us. Imagine my shock when she started yelling to Mum that I had made Anthony throw up in the toilet! He was so green in the face that he couldn't deny I had anything to do with it.

I felt so angry at being wrongfully accused, I did what anyone else would have done to their whiny, pesky and irritating sister. I challenged her to hold the egg on her tongue. The silly girl was so eager to prove she was better than the boys, she swallowed the whole egg! There, it wasn't really my fault, was it? Anthony vomited a second time. Alvin couldn't stop laughing. But I felt really guilty when she asked me what I made her eat. I told her it was a sweet. She said it wasn't sweet at all. Well, I wouldn't know, because I'm not stupid enough to put one in my mouth.

How could you, Amos!
Get rid of those those lizard's eggs!

Wednesday, 6 May

ENTERING A SCIENCE COMPETITION

The principal asked to see me today. I thought I was going to get punished but he said he wanted to submit the A^2SO for a science competition! He also suggested that we could do an issue on sports and science. Hmm... like featuring Michael Phelps and a study of why he can swim so fast? Wow, his face would sell many copies of our magazine!

Thursday, 7 May

BACK TO SWIMMING

On top of brisk walking and jogging, which Coach gets us Slim Club kids to do, I have swimming three times a week. I feel so tired after school some days, and I have tons of homework to do too! How can anyone possibly juggle studies and sports?

Word has been going around in school that Michael is training really hard in swimming. Does he think he's Michael Phelps? He's just Michael Phui. What a joke. But actually, Michael's quite something. His results in class are good, and I know his parents can't afford tuition. So he must be really smart to study on his own. And he's good at balancing studies and sports. How does he do it?

Friday, 8 May

LOST IN SWIMMING!

I CAN'T BELIEVE IT! Michael came in FIRST today at swimming practice! Oh man... I must be struck with bad luck because I played with those blasted condoms!

Alvin picked up Michael Phui's swimming schedule for a peek. He's really serious about training. He hits the pool nine times a week. NINE TIMES!

Three times in the morning on his own before school, three times in the afternoon with us, and three times on his own again on weekends. What is he training for - to be a dolphin? And how does he find the time to study?

Alvin also saw a copy of Michael's diet plan. What kind of freak has a diet plan?

BREAKFAST
- 4 pieces of bread with fried egg, cheese, lettuce, tomatoes, fried onions and mayonnaise.
- 1 piece of pancake with maple syrup.

LUNCH
- Fried noodles with 5 chicken wings and 1 hash brown.
- Spaghetti with tomato sauce and meat balls.
- Fruits and vegetables.

SNACK
- Milk with cheese toast.

DINNER
- Rice with chicken chop.
- Fruit juice.

SUPPER
- Milo with biscuits.

No wonder he's so big-sized! How can anyone eat so much? He's not human. And FRIED ONIONS? All that bad breath. Anthony said he heard that the principal is paying for all of Michael's meals. Looks like the school is serious about grooming him to be a swimming star. Hey, why wasn't I asked?

MICHAEL WANNABE PHELPS

4pm

Michael has been going around challenging everyone to a test of endurance. Not in swimming, but in swallowing goldfish! Seems that Michael Phelps wrote he did that in his book. I'm going to call the SPCA to complain. Today, I saw him go head on with one of the other kids in school – Michael challenged him to hold a goldfish in his mouth for as long as he could. Michael beat the kid – he held it in his mouth for five seconds longer! I'm going to be sick. I don't know what's worse – hearing that the real Michael swallowed a goldfish, or seeing this fake Michael doing a poor imitation.

7pm

I called the SPCA and they wanted to speak to my mum! I called to tell them that a gross, inhumane act was committed in my school against a goldfish. I tried calling the Agri-Food and Veterinary Authority next. They took down my number and said they would call me back. I waited the entire afternoon. They didn't call me back.

BIG STAR IN SCHOOL

2pm

Anthony did what I told him to. He reported Michael's disturbing fish-in-the-mouth act to the principal, but Michael was let off with just a stern warning. That's it? The poor goldfish. All that bad onion breath it had to endure. Michael is a big star in our school now. He gets special treatment during swimming practice and everyone has to wait for him while he does his big business in the toilet. Yup, we have to wait while the king sits on his throne. And he always has to go just before swimming practice. He must believe that this will make him lighter so that he can swim faster.

5pm

Ah Kong called me this afternoon. He said he had bought lots of durians for us. Ah Kong said that when he feels really weak and tired, he would eat durians to perk himself up. Hmm... that makes some sense. Durians are rich in carbohydrates and protein.

DURIANS FOR BREAKFAST, LUNCH AND DINNER

Mum has not been noticing what I have been eating – lots of durians which Ah Kong brought over. Phew, when I burped tonight, I really reeked of pungent durian!

Friday, 15 May

1pm

I can't believe my luck today. I was in the toilet doing big business, when guess who showed up? It was Michael Phui! He had to wait for me, while I did a major bomb. And when I was done, I rushed out without flushing! Poor Michael, I heard him swearing after he slammed the toilet door! Phew, all that awful durian remains!

6pm

Swam my best in weeks today! Michael came in third, after me. The durians must have worked! But guess who came in with the best time? It was Somaly! Looks like she's tougher than I thought.

Tuesday, 19 May

BABY FOR REAL?

11am

Mum had very bad cramps when she woke up. She was wailing so loudly, all our neighbours rushed over! Dad rushed back from work and I followed Mum to the hospital in an ambulance, while Po-Po took WPI to her house to stay over. My baby brother simply loves drama. No one in the family has sat in an ambulance before, not even when Mum gave birth to WPI or me!

Mum was in labour for so long! I drifted in and out of sleep. I finally saw Dad rush back from the delivery ward. He told me Baby was born. I was so relieved, I almost cried. This must be how Alvin felt when his spider babies were born. I saw Mum being wheeled out of the delivery ward, after 12 hours of labour. She sounded hoarse when she said she didn't faint this time. The first two times, when she gave birth to WPI and me, she chose to have an operation, as she couldn't stand the sight of blood. But this time, she had a natural birth, without any pain killer! I thought I heard screams in my sleep... could that have been Mum?

Anyway, I can't believe I'm writing this, my baby brother is being named after a mountain! Really, Mum, you don't have to do this, I'm convinced that women are capable and strong! You can give birth to babies and there are women climbing mountains. But really, Everest Lee?

everest

THE FIRST SINGAPORE WOMEN'S TEAM ON MOUNT EVEREST

Yup, it's all over the news. After five years of training and three days of scaling the mountain, three women have made it to the top of Mount Everest. Amazing.

I know Mum wanted to commemorate this women's achievement. But she didn't have to name my baby brother Everest! Dad has tried to talk Mum out of it, saying men have scaled Everest too, and she could name Baby after one of them.

But no such luck, Mum said Everest is a unique name and it will always remind her of this high moment for Singapore women in mountaineering.

I called Po-Po to tell her about Baby's name. She's a little deaf these days, and she screamed at me, "Why must your mother give her boys ridiculous names? One was named after cookies, and now his brother is named after a battery!"

That's me, Famous Amos. But did I say Eveready? I was yelling "Everest" into the phone so loudly, the nurses walking by all patted me on the back and said, "Your baby brother is so cute!" Yup, only a few hours old and he's already making all the women swoon.

Maybe I should have suggested "Alvin II" instead.

Friday, 22 May

PUTTING KING KONG TO SHAME

11am

Mum made it a point to tell the whole family that two more Singaporean women made it to the top of Mount Everest today. I did some research on the internet and found out that the height of the mountain is 20 times the height of the Empire State Building. King Kong only managed to climb one Empire State, but these women climbed 20!

I need to respect women a little more. I don't think I could even climb to the top of Bukit Timah hill! How do they breathe at that altitude?

This marks an important milestone in my memory of incredible women – five who climbed Mount Everest, and my mother, who gave birth to my baby brother after screaming for 12 hours. Women have amazing lung power.

Mum is back from the hospital. I saw my baby brother's birth certificate. He's officially Everest Lee.

Monday, 25 May

DIDN'T GO FOR SWIMMING

I didn't feel like swimming today, so I faked a note. I scribbled, "Please excuse Amos Lee from practice. He is sick." I signed off with a squiggle. Hope Coach won't ask any questions.

Tuesday, 26 May

COACH VS MUM

Coach called Mum at home. He wanted to know why I missed swimming yesterday. Mum yelled that she just had a baby, so could he please leave her alone. That was really funny! Mum can bark louder than him. "OOOFF, OOOFF, OOOFF!" I also heard her tell him, "My son is not FAT. His bones are heavy!" Aw, poor Coach.

Later on, I felt bad about faking the note, so I told Mum everything. To punish me for lying and forgery, she made me scrub all the tiles on the bathroom floor. With an old toothbrush! Imagine how grossed out I felt when I picked up a clump of hair.

53

It was all Mum's hair. Yeeks, she's going bald! My poor mum, she must be going through a great deal of stress since Everest was born. I shouldn't give her any more trouble.

Monday, 1 June

SWIMMING PRACTICE

It's the school holidays again but Mum is in no state to bring WPI and I out. I can see the stress of taking care of Everest is really getting to her. She keeps calling me Everest, and WPI, Amos. This morning, she forgot to comb her hair, and came out of her bedroom looking

like Medusa!

Anyway, I spent the whole morning at the swimming pool. Coach got into one of his military moods today. He made all of us line up in a row, and marched up and down, talking about working as a team to conquer the enemy. The sun was so hot that by the time he was done, we started shoving each other to get into the water quickly. That only got him yelling at us even more, "Is this your grandfather's pool? Think like soldiers, not monkeys. Take care of one another!" He made all of us climb out of the pool and stand in the hot sun till practice time was over. Can you believe it? We didn't even get to swim today, and all of us went home with a bad sunburn. As I was leaving, I heard him muttering, "Bunch of monkeys! No team spirit!"

Coach is not just crazy, he's seriously misinformed. Monkeys are a great bunch of team mates because they do everything together! But I cannot imagine having to work together with Michael, monkey or not.

Well, whatever it is, I have decided to focus on my training during the holidays. If Michael hopes to be a dolphin, then I will be a sea lion. A monkey I am not!

Wednesday, 3 June

Ah Kong and Po-Po came to visit today. While Po-Po was busy with WPI, Mum got Ah Kong to accompany me to swim at the public pool. I told Ah Kong that I wanted to swim as fast as a sea lion. He was very happy and excited. After I finished my swim, Ah Kong showed me something he wrote down while waiting for me – a training schedule!

I took a look at it and almost DIED! He said I must do cross-training to build my strength and stamina. Every day!

AMOS LEE'S TRAINING SCHEDULE

Monday	20 laps
Tuesday	10 laps + half an hour on the stationary bike + 2 sets of 15 push-ups
Wednesday	School training camp
Thursday	School training camp
Friday	10 laps + half an hour jog + 2 sets of 15 sit-ups
Saturday	School training camp
Sunday	Weightlifting

Oh man... I am beginning to regret telling Ah Kong about this!

Amos, Ah Kong loves you and this sounds like a great schedule for you!

Go for it!

I'm amazed that Mum has time to find my diary while taking care of Everest! Women are really great at multi-tasking! OK Mum, I know you just want me out of the house so that you can focus on Everest. I will give Ah Kong's schedule a try!

Friday, 12 June

TRAINING HELPS!

Ah Kong is usually such a kind, gentle man. But since he became my "personal coach", he has become so fierce! I can't even give Ah Kong a sick note because he knows where I live! Seriously, I have never exercised so much before! But the good news is, thanks to Ah Kong, I have lost 5kg! Guess I won't need to join the Slim Club when school starts! Hurray!

The most interesting thing has also happened to me. I think my male factor has grown a little! I measured it, and it grew by 0.5cm. This is fantastic! Now Michael can't tease me any more!

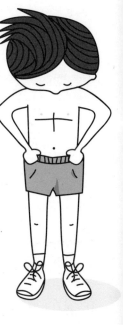

AMOS, I DON'T THINK EXERCISING MAKES YOU GROW DOWN THERE! YOU SHOULDN'T WORRY SO MUCH. IT WILL GROW. TRUST ME, I SHOULD KNOW. — DAD

Mum must have asked Dad to comment on this. Really, what is it with my parents! Shouldn't I be entitled to some privacy?

Monday, 15 June

SWIM MEET

Coach called the swim team down for a friendly competition against a neighbouring school. We knew we were in big trouble when we saw the kids from the other school. They were HUGE and they looked tough and mean. All my confidence and energy from Ah Kong's training disappeared and I felt lousy when we changed into our swimming suits. Things got worse when Michael came over and taunted Alvin, Anthony and I in the changing room. He called us weak and said he was going to beat us all! I almost punched him but as Coach was around, I didn't want to get into trouble. By the time the match started, the 3As were all feeling quite down.

We swam terribly today. Michael got trounced by the boys from the other school. Somaly didn't do well in the Girls' Division either. And, as for the 3As, we were all disqualified, for jumping into the pool before the horn went off. The one time we were all united, it was for a false start. Arrgh!

There was one boy from the other school that caught our attention. He was so huge, and his arms were so long! He looked like he ate horses for lunch. He was really fast too. Awesome, in fact. But this boy had a really bad attitude. He spat in Michael's lane when he got out of the water. I could see that Michael was furious. For once, I sympathised with him. For being humiliated because he was the slower swimmer.

DRESSING DOWN BY COACH

Coach spoke to all of us today. He was really upset with our performance yesterday and listed our strengths and weaknesses:

MICHAEL – hungry for success, serious in training. But he was scolded for provoking his team mates again and again. He has no respect for others.

ALVIN – always thinking about girls. If he could channel his attention to training, he would do well as he has natural talent.

ANTHONY – Mama's boy. He has to prove to his mother that he can stand up for himself.

And as for me, Coach said I have to stop clowning around and be serious in my life for a change.

He ended his pep talk by yelling at us, "Your enemy is within! Overcome it!" Really, I think he should lighten up. This is about swimming. We are NOT in the army!

DISAPPOINTMENT AT HOME

Ah Kong was upset with me. He said seeing that I didnt care about failing in the swim meet was worse than losing the competition. Even Mum said I'm not serious enough to want to win. Huh? What's that supposed to mean? What is wrong with everyone? This is about swimming, not life and death! So what if I don't care about losing or winning? Big deal.

Everyone is crazy!

Friday, 19 June

POETRY IN THE TOILET
BY AMOS LEE

Bit by bit, drop by drop
An outpouring comes
A complete melt down
There, a big puddle forms
It's all spent
Tears from within

Saturday, 20 June

BABIES AND MILK

10am

Everest is getting to be a big baby. To think that he was so small and feeble at birth. Mum is getting more stressed because she says her milk just can't keep up with demand. I'm not sure what that means.

All I know is that poor Everest is always wailing for Mum

to breastfeed him. Mum has to drop everything she's doing, rush into the bedroom and feed Everest in bed. When they emerge after 30 minutes, both would be sweating. Mum because she had been told no air-conditioning after childbirth, and Everest because he had to suck so hard for milk. My poor baby brother.

12pm

ALL ABOUT BREAST MILK

According to the big book on Conception, Pregnancy and Birth, a woman who has just given birth is able to breastfeed as there are milk-secreting glands in her breasts. During pregnancy, the body releases hormones which stimulate the glands to produce colostrum. Colostrum provides baby with water, protein, sugar, vitamins, minerals and antibodies to protect against infection. Three to five days after the baby is born, milk production replaces colostrum. For as long as baby breastfeeds, there shall be enough milk!

Wow, Mum can offer serious competition to a cow!

Sunday, 21 June

MUM, THE MOO-MI QUEEN

Mum has been pumping out lots of breast milk. Our fridge is now filled with bottles of her milk, labelled by dates. I can't even keep ice cream in the fridge now, as Mum's breast milk is moving to the freezer compartment. I seriously suspect Mum is using her breast milk to wash her face. She looked guilty when I saw her washing her face with whitish, murky liquid from a basin. I even saw Mum offering WPI cereal for breakfast, lunch and dinner. With suspicious-looking milk.

Whose? Cow or human? Yucks! My mother has become a psycho!

ME, A DIAPER TRACKER

A crisis! Everest hasn't been able to pass motion. It's been a week! Now Mum wants me to track his diaper content. Looks like I can't escape this new chore since swimming practices have been cancelled to give us all a break from training!

DIAPER CHART

22 June	Day 8
Morning, Pee x 5 - Clear	
Noon, Pee x 3 - Yellow	
Night, Pee x 2 - I can't tell the colour!	
23 June	Day 9
Morning, Pee x 4 - All yellow	
Noon and Night, Pee x 8 - Yellow and GROSS!	

I'm getting really tired of doing this! And the diapers are so smelly. I feel like vomiting!

Wednesday, 24 June

9am

WPI offered to track the diapers. Great! I'm off to play computer games finally!

7pm

I shouldn't have trusted her. I saw only four soiled diapers in the dustbin. Poor Everest, he's got a rash from all that urine trapped on his bum! My sister is really wicked. Mum tried feeding Everest a tiny bit of mashed pumpkin pulp today. Hmmm... will this work?

9pm

Thought I saw Everest scrunching his face. So quick?

10pm

I asked WPI to check Everest's diaper. She fell for it. She ripped open the diaper and let out a scream! Nine days' worth of human waste and pumpkin remains tumbled out. Serves her right!

Monday, 29 June

THE ASIAN YOUTH GAMES

It's back to school again. Today, Coach had an exciting announcement for us - he managed to get us tickets to watch some of the Asian Youth Games events! The AYG is being held as a lead up to the world's first Youth Olympic Games, which Singapore is hosting in 2010. I think this is Coach's ploy to get us into the spirit of sports. Another one of his psycho-lo-gi-cal mind games!

A SOCCER MATCH

We went to the Jalan Besar Stadium to watch a soccer match between Singapore and China. I don't really understand why, since we are swimmers, not soccer players! But it was an incredible match – 22 football players running around on the pitch, chasing the ball. Oh man, it was so hot, but the players didn't seem to mind. All that sweat! I had goose bumps just watching them fight for the goals. Singapore lost 0-3, to China.

Amos, did you know that the Jalan Besar Stadium was the birthplace of Singapore football?

I need a lock and key to keep Mum from reading my diary. I hid this in my underwear drawer and she could still find it!

A WRITTEN ASSIGNMENT

Coach asked us to write a composition on our thoughts about the soccer match. I thought this was a bit silly, since we are swimmers, not sports reporters! I just wrote down whatever came to mind, and when Coach read my composition, to my surprise, he said mine was the best composition in the entire swim team. Coach said I write better than I swim! I can't decide if that is a compliment, or an insult!

Here is what I wrote:

THE LIONS VS. THE DRAGONS
by AMOS LEE

In the mythical battle of lion against dragon, who has the upper hand? The lion may have the loudest roar, but the dragon exhales fire that can quell that roar. Burn is worse than bite!

The soccer match between Singapore and China taught me something. A competition is about having stamina, plus something else – the will to win. Skills can be trained and acquired, which can lead to impressive stamina, but the will to win comes from a deeper desire in competitors. Only they know if they have it in them to fight and win.

Coach wrote in BIG, BOLD letters across my paper, "DO YOU HAVE THE FIRE, AMOS?" First, he talks about the enemy, next he wants fire. Maybe he should go back to the army.

Wednesday, 8 July

SINGAPORE GIRLS TRIUMPH AT AYG!

My theory is proven right again. Out of the nine golds Singapore got at the AYG, five were for swimming and they were all won by girls. Women have amazing lung power. They start their training from young!

Friday, 10 July

SECOND WRITTEN ASSIGNMENT

Coach said he wanted us to write a cheer for the team. The best cheer would be used by the school's cheering squad, to support us at swim meets. He said there wasn't enough cheering going on at the AYG. The athletes needed the support from spectators to keep them going strong. This is easy enough. I wrote mine in five minutes:

KILL! KILL! KILL!
Hit them, break them,
throw them in the pool!
We want to have some
RED, HOT BLOOD!

A SPORTS STAR!

Coach arranged for us to visit the newly opened Sengkang Recreation Centre. It had excellent facilities. We had the best time training this afternoon! Imagine our surprise when we met a sports star. At first, we had no idea who she was. But we saw her swimming and boy, she was really fast! We should have guessed she was someone important, as there were a couple of photographers waiting around, snapping shots at her. When the swimmer surfaced, Michael shrieked, "It's Tao Li!" Wow!

Tao Li was really nice. She popped over to talk to us. She encouraged us to keep on training. We even had our picture taken with her. So cool! Made my day seeing a sports star training. And she really was just like one of us!

A Sports Heroine!
Women Power!

Really, Mum should meet Coach. They would be the best of friends. I have almost given up trying to hide my diary. I hid it in my pillow, and she could still find it!

ALL ABOUT CHEERS

Coach passed around all the cheers written by the swimming team. We had a good time reading and laughing at all of them. Some were so badly written!

Imagine this:
Knock! Knock!
Who's There?
We Are The Swim Champs!

Another one:
Fork and Spoon!
Stab and Scoop!
Swim Like A Fish!
What, are we in the restaurant business?

And some joker even wrote a speech!
Are We Ready?
Should We Try?
Can We Do It?
Yes, We Can!

I laughed the loudest when Coach read this out. He was really angry with me. He said HE wrote it! Oh man, just my luck. He said it was adapted from a speech made by America's President Barack Obama. Sheesh... how was I supposed to know!

He yelled at me, "See that big tree? Go run and touch it and come back!" The tree must have been at least 1 km from where we sat! That was a 2 km run for laughing at him.

Really, he's a psycho!

It's psychopath, Amos. And it was a really inspiring speech by President Obama. Standing against all odds, can we overcome them? Yes, we can!

I think Mum and Coach may be related. I have run out of ideas on where to hide this!

Saturday, 25 July

THE NE SHOW

We got to attend the National Day Parade today! Unlike last year when our school had to perform in the NDP, it was a nice change to be part of the audience this year.

The parade was like a big theatre production, with songs, dances, giant puppet and lion dance performances, and the usual parade march. But what I loved most was getting the fun pack. With lots of freebies! Cool!

The best part was seeing the para-shoo-tits and the military fly-past. Coach leapt to attention like a soldier,

with his chest pushed out and his stomach sucked in!
He even looked like he was crying a little as we sang the
National Anthem!

*The NDP sounds like it was great fun! There's a lot
to be thankful for, Amos – our country and home, a
bright future for our children! And it's parachutists!
Use a dictionary.*

I stuck this diary behind the mirror on the wall and she
could still find it! Amazing.

Wednesday, 29 July

STRAY CAT IN THE HOUSE!

I SHOULD HAVE KNOWN WPI WOULD BE UP TO HER
TRICKS AGAIN. She brought home a stray cat this
afternoon! Instead of ordering WPI to let the cat go,
Mum has been spending the past few hours helping WPI
think of a name for it. This is so unfair! Mum did not allow
me to keep my baby spider,
but when WPI brings
home a stray animal
that nobody wants, it
is welcomed as
part of the
Lee Family!

You know, I can think of a couple of names for this animal – Sly-Mew, Vermin-Face, Decepti-Cat, Stupidi-Kit!

10pm

They named her Feline. How original.

Saturday, 1 August

On top of taking care of the laundry, I have also been tasked to clean the kitty litter and help WPI warm milk for Vermin Face's feed. Mum said it was dangerous for WPI to use the microwave or handle hot water so I will have to do all that! Fantastic, so I am also the Guardian of the Microwave and Chief Handler of the Thermos.

And, How Much Milk Can Decepti-Cat Drink? Lots! For something with such a small stomach, she sure can drink by the bucket! WPI was bugging me the whole day to fix up the cat's milk. And it had to be really precise – two parts evaporated milk to one part water, mixed in a cup. Then, steep the cup in a bowl of hot water to warm it. Feline drank at least sixteen portions of milk today!

I know, because I counted the number of times I had to pour the hot water out from the thermos flask. My arm hurts even as I dig my nose now.

COLD NIGHT FOR STUPIDI-KIT

WPI woke me up at 2am this morning to ask me to warm her cat! For a moment, I thought she wanted me to put the cat in the microwave. That woke me up immediately. But I heard wrong – she was asking for a bottle of hot water. She used a towel to wrap the bottle, and then placed it beside the cat, like a bolster. Amazing, such budding maternal instincts.

Thursday, 6 August

THE CAT CAN SHOOT ITS PEE!

We have a blooming genius cat living in the house. This morning, I saw the cat climb onto the toilet bowl, perch itself on its hind legs, and then shoot its pee into the bowl! So we've been misled. It's not a She-Cat. It's a Tom-Cat. No wonder the kitty litter is always clean and dry!

After dinner, I saw him peeing on one of the curtains.

I yelled for Mum immediately, and of course, she was furious. Hmm... this gives me an idea.

Saturday, 8 August

THE CAT IS NOW CALLED TOM! – ALL ABOUT CAT PEE

I had to be really patient in coaxing Tom to pee in the kitty litter pan. He was suspicious of me, and I don't blame him. All it took was one whiff of tuna, and Tom was hooked! I collected enough urine.

Mum was really upset today. She said she could smell cat pee everywhere! Finally, she decided in the evening that Tom had to leave. Actually, I only sprinkled some pee on her potted plants and shoes. But it did the trick. She thought Tom

peed all over the house heh heh heh! WPI was really upset and cried very loudly, "Feline's my baby! Feline's my baby!" But Mum was firm. I think Mum felt sorry for WPI, but she made Tom leave.

I am just glad that I don't have to warm milk and clean poop anymore! I'm sure WPI will get over this. It's just a cat, after all.

BACK TO TRAINING

Training at the pool, I enjoy watching how other schools field their swimming teams. We met the Goliath of Swimming again. I found out that he was called Bif. His school always has a team at the pool, training for either individual boys' or girls' races, or as a relay team. I enjoy watching the boys' medley relay team train - you pick the best swimmers in the school and put the strongest individuals in backstroke, butterfly, breaststroke and freestyle together. I can see that they are serious about training. Really focused.

Our school has never fielded a relay team in any of the inter-school competitions. We just don't have enough good swimmers. And we lack the team spirit that would stand up against a team like Bif's.

BIF

Saw Bif again at the pool this afternoon. I noticed that he has a peculiar habit before swimming. He always scratches his crotch. He does it discreetly, but because I was watching him, I saw it.

What a sight! I nudged Somaly, who happened to be standing beside me. She nudged Alvin, who nudged Anthony and all of us started giggling. Bif heard us. He turned, glared at us, then made a rude sign. What a terrible thing to do!

When the horn blew, Bif was the first to jump off the block. He hit the water like a dolphin, and swam two full body lengths under water before breaking the surface. It was a 4 x 100m medley relay. I have never seen such excellent team spirit before! The crowd was on their feet, cheering the boys on. Bif gave his team a good run. It was an incredible performance!

Oh man... we really are up against water machines. If Michael Phui thinks he's Phelps, then Bif is Ian Thorpe. I think I finally understand what it takes to win a race - you need lots of talent, and team spirit. Our school doesn't have it.

Amos IS a spidybabynologist! BWHA HA HA

HOW TERRIBLE!

The last few days were the worst in my life! I lost my diary. It must have happened during swimming practice. And which Vermin-Face wrote in MY diary!!!!!!!!!! Wait till I get my hands on the culprit. I will pluck every hair from his body. I found my diary in one of the lockers at the pool and there was a note saying, "Return to Amos Lee."

Could it be Michael? He has been telling the whole school that I love spiders. Today, he passed out posters with his face printed on them, with a tagline that screamed, "Michael, An Olympic Dream!" Did he get the idea from my diary? The principal said to write about Michael Phelps, not the wannabe!

Or maybe it's Somaly? Maybe she's jealous that the 3As are back together and Alvin hangs out with me now? But then again, Alvin still hangs out with her quite a lot. And she said she loves my writing! She said I'm funny and have a real talent. Maybe she stole my diary to read more of my writing?

A TERRIBLE DAY

Met Bif at the pool today. What rotten luck. He challenged me to a swim. He said I could choose to swim any style. With twenty girls and boys looking on at us, it was hard for me to turn him down.

We swam. I lost. But that wasn't all. Bif came out of the pool and stood at my lane, waiting for me to finish. As I reached the end of the pool and took off my goggles, he made a "LOSER" sign and started yelling at me, calling me weak and sissy. Alvin and Anthony came over and Bif called us all losers, telling us to "balek kampong" as this pool had no room for losers.

It was so humiliating. The last insult was when Bif called me a freak and said, "Amos, you're a SPIDYSEXNOLOGIST!" Yup, he was the one who stole my diary. Bif even asked me to crawl between his legs! I shoved him and we got into a fight. Good thing Alvin and Anthony were there to stop Bif from beating me up any further. I got a bruised upper lip from a punch. But I think my ego was even more crushed. I cried on the way home. Lucky I had money with me to take a cab. The driver asked why I was crying. I told him my pet died.

I WANT TO QUIT!

I have never felt so terrible in my life before. I really want to quit swimming. It's not worth the humiliation of being ridiculed.

Friday, 4 September

COACH'S PEP TALK

I didn't go for swimming practice today. And I didn't give Coach a sick note either. I just didn't feel like going.

In the evening, Coach called me up. He said he had heard about the confrontation at the pool. He told me he was sorry Bif was so nasty. He said Bif was being groomed in the national Under-14 swimming team, for the Youth Olympic Games. I couldn't believe anyone with such a bad attitude could be chosen for the national team. Coach said because Bif was hungry enough, he made it his goal to be the best in swimming. Coach also said that he had decided to field an all boys' team from our school for the inter-school freestyle relay competition. Coach said he wanted me to be part of the relay team. But, I said no. Coach seemed disappointed but he didn't say anything. I cried again after we put down the phone. What is wrong with me? I'm turning into a wimp!

Saturday, 5 September

Exams are after the one-week break. Must concentrate on my studies. I'm through with swimming!

TOM IS BACK!

This afternoon I found a cat waiting outside our flat!
It was Tom. Everyone was excited to see him, except
Everest and me. The baby cried when he saw Tom, and
I just rolled my eyes.

Mum said, "Let's just feed Tom when he visits, shall we?"
I think she has a soft spot for stray cats. Dad said that
he heard there was a psychopath going round our block
of flats. Stray cats have been found drugged and tied up.
The mad man must really hate stray cats. Two have died,
when they didn't wake up from being drugged. I heard Mum
mumbling to Dad something about it being good for WPI to
have a pet to take care of, now that Everest is born.

TOM GOES MISSING

11am

Strange, Tom didn't visit today. I went to see our second floor neighbour. I've seen her feeding Tom at times. She said she didn't see Tom.

6pm

I called the SPCA to report a missing cat. They said they don't run a Missing Cat Search service. I tried calling the Agri-Food and Veterinary Authority next. They took down our number and said they would call back. I waited the entire afternoon but they didn't call me back.

WPI is so upset, she refused to eat her dinner. Now she's lying on the sofa crying non-stop. Actually, I am a little worried too. I asked Mum if I could call the police. She freaked out when I said that. She suggested that I form a search party to look for Tom tomorrow.

Wednesday, 9 September

Anthony, Alvin and Somaly came over this afternoon to help look for Tom. WPI joined us as well. I told them that I'm only doing this because I don't want the psychopath to get Tom. When I mentioned, "the psychopath", WPI started crying and Mum got upset with me. "I'm sure Tom is perfectly fine!" Mum yelled.

We searched for three hours around the estate. No Tom! Where could he be? I don't think I can sleep tonight.

TOM, FOUND!

Oh man... we found Tom
today. He was left in a
rubbish dump, barely
alive. His front paw
had been badly tied up
with rubber bands! It's
inhumane! We didn't dare
to cut the bands as his
paw looked badly infected.
Mum rushed Tom to the
SPCA, while Po-Po came

over to take care of Everest. Poor Tom – he looked so
lifeless! The SPCA officer said Tom might have to be put
down. WPI and Mum cried when they heard the news.
We had to leave him behind. I felt awful.

Friday, 11 September

6pm

The SPCA called and said they had found a vet willing
to do surgery for Tom! But his paw would have to be
amputated. We rushed down immediately to see the vet.
The surgery took two hours.

Alvin, Somaly and Anthony came over to the hospital
after their swimming practice. We took a taxi home with
Tom in a box. He was on a portable drip which we got from
the vet. The vet said Tom was un-con-scious, which is a
bit like sleeping, only we're not sure when he will wake up.
Mum showed me how to change the bag of drips.

Tom looks really frail, hooked up to a bag of drip and with his eyes closed like that. WPI asked when Tom would wake up. Mum and Dad just hugged her.

10pm

I have been looking at Tom sleeping. Maybe there is a way to help him wake up faster...

11pm

Tom stirred when I placed a can of tuna near his face. Mum came in and asked me what I was doing, so I had to explain to her that I had used a can of tuna to coax Tom to pee before.

Then, I decided to confess about how I had dripped Tom's pee over her plants and shoes, so that she would get rid of him. I think Mum could tell I felt really bad about that. She just asked me to get some sleep.

Saturday, 12 September

6am

I couldn't sleep so I got up to take a look at Tom again. I tried barking at him. "Woof, woof... WOOF, WOOF, WOOF!" He opened one eye to look at me! Then, I tried a gentler bark. "Yip, yip... YIP, YIP, YIP!" It worked! Tom opened both eyes to look at me.

Everyone woke up when they heard crying. Nope, it wasn't Everest. It was Amos from ALL the anxiety and concern for a cat. Yup, I cried buckets when Tom woke up finally.

Now I know how Alvin felt about his spider babies. WPI said she thought she heard a dog in the house, but I told her she was being silly.

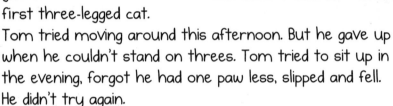

I'm now the official guardian of the world's first three-legged cat.

Tom tried moving around this afternoon. But he gave up when he couldn't stand on threes. Tom tried to sit up in the evening, forgot he had one paw less, slipped and fell. He didn't try again.

Sunday, 13 September

Anthony checked on the internet and found a private animal clinic that offers therapy for animals who have been injured in accidents. I thought it was a clever idea to get help for Tom. Mum brought the 3As and Tom to the clinic and we accompanied him as he was taught to jump, crawl and kick around with one paw less. It was just like old times, the 3As back together, united in helping Tom to get strong!

When we got home, Somaly came over. She put together a nice box, with cute toys and a pretty blanket for Tom to sleep in. I felt so touched. I guess that's what friends are for, giving one another support.

I guess I shouldn't be angry with Somaly for stealing Alvin, after all she makes an effort to be part of our group and she's kind of cool.

MORE VISITORS!

The media came to our house today! They wanted to see for themselves how a victim of the Cat Mangler survived a vicious prank. Yup, the psychopath got caught. I hope they cut off his leg as well.

FAMOUS AMOS

Oh man... my picture appeared in the newspapers today. There was a small story on the Cat Mangler and I was quoted as saying, "An Eye For An Eye, Cut His Leg Off!" They said I was a devoted owner who cried when he thought his beloved pet was going to die. SO EMBARRASSING! They must have spoken to Mum!

And I thought no one would read the small column in the newspapers. Guess what? I finally got a call from the Agri-Food and Veterinary Authority. They tracked me down and wanted to know if I had an animal licence for my cat.

I told them to call my mother and hung up the phone. When they called again, I heard Mum screaming at them, "Don't you have better things to do?" Yup, I don't think they will be calling again.

FOOD REFUSAL

9am

Yippee! Exams are over so I get to rest at home today, instead of study. Computer games here I come!

6pm

Mum looked flustered at lunch and told us we had a serious problem – Tom has been refusing his food for three days! He was taken off the drip a long time ago, but had only been drinking a little milk. If this goes on, he would not have any energy to run around on threes. WPI said Tom looked so listless and down, despite having so much milk and tuna being offered to him.

Alvin, Somaly and Anthony came over after lunch and we decided to spy on Tom to see what was going on. At first, Tom just lay there. His milk and tuna were in front of him, but he just closed his eyes. Then something interesting happened. He got up and started sniffing around the cupboards in our house. Maybe he could smell something?

He did look hungry, but what was he looking for? He walked past his food and headed for the cupboards instead. At that moment, a little lizard made an appearance, and Tom got all excited. He forgot he had three legs, sprang onto Mum's stove and tried to make a jump for the lizard. Silly, the lizard could climb walls, and Tom was no Spider Cat. He only had three legs!

Next, we saw him waiting patiently for the lizard to appear. And it did! It peeped its head out from behind the cupboard, took one look at Tom and disappeared behind it. Tom went mad! He sprang onto the cupboard and tried to stick his paw behind it. Nope, he couldn't reach it. Tom must have felt humiliated, being made fun of by a lizard!

Tom waited patiently for the lizard to appear. This time, he hid under the table. After a while, our little friend appeared. Tom waited till the lizard crawled out from behind the cupboard to move lower down the wall. Then he sprang out from under the table and did a spectacular jump to swipe the lizard off the wall. The lizard fell to the floor and scuttled away. But it couldn't outrun a hungry cat. Tom stopped it with his paw, flipped it over on its back and wrestled it with one paw before taking his time to swallow the lizard whole. WOW!

Fire in the will to kill! Maybe I should write about this in A²SO! And oh yes... I will NEVER kiss Tom ever again for the rest of my life.

ISSUE #2

A² SO

The Amos & Anthony **Science Observer**

THE STORY OF TOM AND THE LIZARD

BY AMOS LEE

I am writing about the hunger and fire in the will of a cat.

I have a pet, Tom, who had his leg amputated recently. He lost all fighting spirit and almost died because he felt sorry for himself, and didn't want to eat or drink.

It took a lizard to wake him up, a prey which stirred the deep hunting instinct in this cat!

For many weeks when we had Tom, we used to feed him tuna from a can, and milk warmed in a microwave. Tom got used to the good life and became complacent. He was tricked by a psychopath who lured him with poisoned food.

Tom had lost his animal instinct and trusted a stranger. He got one paw tied up with multiple rubber bands, which cut off his blood flow. The paw became infected, which led to it being removed.

When we brought Tom to the vet, he was barely breathing. After he came home from the operation, it took him almost 12 hours before he woke up.

No amount of love or attention was enough to get him through this dark time. Tom found it in himself. It was a lizard that brought the fighter out in him. After three days of going without food, Tom found the reason to scheme and hunt – to capture a lizard and eat it alive.

The moral of the story is that with hunger and fire in the will, we can awaken a hunting instinct to kill.

Sunday, 27 September

SECOND ISSUE OF A²SO

I showed Alvin and Anthony my article about Tom and the Lizard and they both laughed. They said it would sell better than the first issue. I hope so! I really want to save enough money to buy a handphone. We printed 100 copies of A²SO to sell.

Only a handful of kids stopped to look at our magazine.
We managed to sell five copies – all to teachers!
What's happening?

I brought home 94 copies of A²SO.
Sold five and gave one away. The
school cleaner said she likes cats.
I'm so disappointed with sales.

Thursday, 1 October

MY BIRTHDAY! I'M 11 TODAY!

Dad brought us out for a wonderful meal. But we ate
quickly, as we wanted to be home to check on Tom. Alvin,
Anthony and some other classmates called to wish me
Happy Birthday. Everyone asked after Tom. He's so famous
now! Mum got me a pair of swimming
trunks as a present. But I asked her,
what for? I told her, "I won't be
swimming anymore."

Later on, Dad came
by my room and
we had a long talk.
I suspect he knew
about Bif and the
fight I got into –
after all, I'm sure
Mum has been

reading my diary all this while - but it felt good to tell him about everything that had happened, and why I did not want to swim any longer. Dad said he was proud of my swimming skills and asked me to re-consider quitting. He said, "If you focus, I'm sure you can be a great swimmer! Don't be discouraged! And don't let others discourage you!"

I told Dad I would think about what he said.

Alvin called me a second time to ask if I was really sure about quitting swimming. I said I haven't really made up my mind.

Friday, 2 October

ENTERING A COMPETITION AGAIN

The principal asked to see me. He said he had enjoyed reading my article on Tom and offered to send the second issue of A²SO for another competition, since the first issue didn't win a Science award. I said sure, but told him the second issue was selling very poorly. When I told Anthony what the principal said, he was also skeptical that we would win anything. But, no harm trying...

Tuesday, 6 October

FOUNDER'S DAY

It was our school's Founder's Day today. We celebrated it by having a gallery opened in honour of our local sports heroes. Must be another one of Coach's ideas! But what

C. Kunalan

was really interesting was a visit by a former Olympian, who is now a Professor of Physical Education and Sports Science. His name is C. Kunalan. Coach said he was a sprint champion from 1966 to 1970. He ran 100m in 10.3 seconds. Wow, imagine that!

The speaker recounted his experience in coaching athletes in running. He said all athletes have to learn to overcome the enemy within. That's what Coach said too! He said some athletes had natural talent, but lacked confidence, or did not have the hunger to excel. He also shared that it took an athlete a minimum of five years of training before he reached a peak in performance. Wow, that's a lot of training hours!

What was also inspiring was to hear that Kunalan's daughter, Mona, was also a successful athlete who had done Singapore proud in sprinting.

It was a really useful session. Seeing a sports hero being so devoted to his sport and even inspiring his daughter to run made me feel motivated to go back to swimming. I have only just started swimming competitively, for less than a year. So, maybe I shouldn't let Bif get to me? I think I should pick up swimming from where I left off. I have many more years ahead of me.

After the Founder's Day celebration, I bumped into Coach

and told him that I was ready to be part of the boys' relay team. Alvin and Anthony were also with Coach. Everyone gave me high fives! I was surprised when Coach barked out, "Recruits! You will do me proud, you hear!" The 3As jumped to attention and saluted Coach. He seemed really pleased.

He's a real softie at heart. That's our Coach.

That's good, Amos. I think you've matured. You were very brave not to tell me about the fight. And you did well in standing up to the bully. But fighting doesn't resolve a problem. Please remember that, ok?

I thought I was so smart to leave this in the drawer with the dictionary. It's the last place she thinks I would touch, but she found my diary still! My amazing mother!

Friday, 9 October

COACH'S ORDERS

Coach showed up for practice holding 94 copies of A²SO today! He said Anthony had sold it to him for a "bulk discount!" Coach said he had read my article and wanted to use what I wrote to teach the swimming team about mental training. Each of us were given five copies. The instructions from Coach were to put the article up in five places - our locker, on the walls beside our bed and study table, on the door of our fridge, and in the toilet. We must think "hunger and will to kill" each time we swim, sleep, study, eat and pee.

But he also said we mustn't tell our parents that we want to kill. It's just a metaphor for winning.

Coach also showed us a huge picture of a three-legged cat, in swimming trunks and goggles. It was a hilarious picture, but we all got the idea. Oh man, Tom, the three-legged cat, is now the swimming team's mascot, and he doesn't even like to get wet!

I drew the 3As with Tom on my copy of the A²SO. The three Mouseketeers, with whiskers and claws. "EEEEEAUUUIWWWWW!" We will scratch our enemy's eyes out in the pool!

Oops, wrong spelling, Musketeers! See, I figured that if I start using the dictionary, Mum may stop reading my diary.

FACEBOOK

Anthony set up a Facebook account for me. Hey, I didn't ask for one. He lied about my age – entering it as 18. That's not honest, is it? Anthony said he'll be using my Facebook account to blast messages about the Science Observer. Apparently, orders are coming in. "How much are you selling them for?" I asked. He said $2 for the issue on making babies and $0.50 for Tom's story.

Monday, 12 October

11am

As of this morning, Anthony has orders for 300 copies of the first issue. And how about Tom's story? Five, all from members of the Cat Welfare Society. There was also a request from a girl, who said she wanted to meet me. What for? Anthony said he didn't know, but since she's paying $100 for 50 copies of A²SO, it was the least I could do.

6pm

What a HORRIBLE day! The "girl" who asked to meet me turned out to be a middle-aged lady with yellow buck teeth. She was so gross! She kept scratching her armpits as I was signing my name on copies of the Science Observer. Just before I left, she pinched my cheeks and almost left imprints on them with her dirty fingernails! Yucks!

She also asked if I could do a delivery to her home the next time she placed an order. I told her that the magazine was folding. Both Anthony and I would be too busy swimming to produce any more issues.

Got a call from Anthony. He checked the lady's online profile and found out she runs a tuition centre. Whatever! She shouldn't have faked her profile. Under "Age", she put herself as "Sweet 18". I scolded Anthony today, "See, you never know what sort of pervert you will meet online!"

Anthony apologised and said he would remove my Facebook account and cancel all remaining orders for the Science Observer. We made $100 from selling it. We also learnt something about not trusting online profiles of strangers. I spent almost ten minutes scrubbing my cheeks out with Mum's facial wash. Just the thought of being pinched makes me want to vomit. My face is so red and raw now!

Amos, this is really serious. You're lucky that the lady is not some psychopath! You could have been kidnapped! You shouldn't have met strangers from the internet.

And you are too young to be on Facebook!

Right, Mum. I won't dare do this again. Even hiding this under my mattress is not safe. She is STILL reading my diary!

TRAINING FOR REAL!

Alvin, Anthony and I made a pact to swim ten hours a week after our exams. We will focus on studying first. I showed them the training schedule that Ah Kong drew up, and they said they were willing to try it out. With support from one another, I know we can do better in training. Alvin asked if Somaly could join us too. I agreed. Alvin said he hoped Ah Kong's schedule will help him build muscles. Anthony asked if the training would make him look less nerdy. I can't believe my friends are so vain in wanting to look good! This is about swimming better! Oh man...

Friday, 16 October

COACH'S OLYMPIC LESSON

Coach made us play basketball today but he invented a new rule. He said we could only use one arm each. We had to tuck the other arm behind our backs. It was really silly

47

running around, dribbling the ball with one hand. Most of the time, we were too caught up with controlling it, and failed to see the opponent approaching to grab our ball. After a while, Alvin, Anthony and I realised we needed to team up. I was in charge of dribbling, while Anthony looked out for opponents. Alvin was pretty good with scoring, so I would pass him the ball when the three of us moved nearer to the net. We moved as a threesome and it was difficult for our opponents to break us up. We managed to score four times and won the game! Oh man... it was so tough playing with just one arm, but with team work, we did it!

Coach wanted us to think about the values of the game. He said the 3As had shown great team spirit by working together, watching out for one another's back, and by playing fair, with integrity too. No one cheated. We stuck to the rules of the game, and every player used only one arm. He called us all Olympians. We felt proud of our game today. The good news is that Coach said the 3As are all ready to be part of the boys' relay team. Hurray!

Sunday, 18 October

Mum said no more writing in the diary for the next week. It's my final year EXAMS!

A FOOTBALL MATCH

8am

Exams are over! The 3As wanted to hit the pool today, but no such luck - our school is involved in a friendly inter-school football match and it is compulsory for everybody to attend! The weirdest thing is that the game is for girls! I've never heard of girls playing football before! Alvin said he is going to cheer Somaly on. What? Somaly plays football?

5pm

Wow, Somaly can play football! She was in the game today, and what a match it was! She may be small, but boy, can she run! She played like a true lion - fast, ferocious and full of lung power. Really cool! Our team's proudest moment came when a girl from the other school stuck out her leg to trip Somaly. Somaly fell over and landed flat on her face! But she clawed her way back to win the match with a penalty kick. We won 1-0 today! The entire stadium erupted into cheers when the ball went in. Imagine that, a female football heroine! Winning feels FANTASTIC! For once, Alvin wasn't the only one hugging Somaly - everybody was hugging her and patting her on the back, including me!

I should really respect girls more. Not only can they climb mountains and give birth to babies, they are also the best swimmers and can play football too. Enough said.

Monday, 26 October

OUR FIRST BOYS' RELAY TEAM

The football match did something for the school. It ignited a school spirit and a desire in all of us to win. Today, Coach made four of us train together as our school's first boys' relay team – the 3As and Michael. About 200 kids from our school came down to cheer us on. Anyone watching would have thought a competition was going on!

Bif's school was also training at the pool. We saw the entire team stop their poolside push-ups, just to watch us swim. Michael went in first, followed by Anthony, me, then Alvin. Oh man... I can feel my hair standing on ends even as I write this. The spectators chanted:

KILL! KILL! KILL!
HIT THEM, BREAK THEM, THROW THEM IN THE POOL!
WE WANT TO HAVE SOME RED, HOT BLOOD!

Alvin was so fast today, he had all the spectators screaming on their feet! I saw Bif looking really worried when he checked the clock on the wall. Alvin rounded up the relay in under five minutes.

It feels good to have my cheer picked for the cheering squad! Looks like Coach's strategy of getting supporters to push us works. The school spirit has never been stronger! We are ready for the inter-school swimming meet!

Tuesday, 27 October

A²SO WINS AN AWARD!

12pm

I can't believe it! Teacher just told me that the second issue of A²SO has won an award! I told Anthony, "See, some topics sell and others win awards." I wonder what the prize is?

3pm

I CAN'T BELIEVE IT! WE WON HANDPHONE VOUCHERS!

Friday, 30 October

MY FIRST HANDPHONE

After school today, Mum brought
Anthony and I to pick out our
first handphones! So exciting!
The vouchers were nearly enough
for us to buy two basic models
- we just had to use some of the money we made from
selling the Science Observer to top up. Imagine, my first
handphone! Finally! I got a Samsung handphone. Really
neat, with a large touch screen and lots of exciting games.
It even had a cool ring tone and a recordable "answer me"
function. Anthony got a Sony Ericsson handphone.

I gave out my number to everyone at the pool and asked
them to call me. I can't wait to receive my first call.

Monday, 2 November

PHONE IN ACTION

Got a call today. Someone was trying to sell me insurance.
I told him I wasn't even 12, and he hung up on me. So rude!

Wednesday, 4 November

PRANK CALL

A Pizza Hut guy sent a pizza to the principal's office
today. The order was placed with my handphone number!

Horror of horrors. I didn't order any pizza! It must have been a prank call!

The principal was really mad with me. He said if I delivered pizza to him again, he would make me pay for it. This time round, he paid for the pizza, and the teachers had it for tea. Yup, only the teachers, not the students. Sheesh...

Friday, 6 November

BIF THE PRANK CALLER

Found out who ordered the pizza. It was Bif. He asked me at the pool today if the pizza was too cold to eat. I got Bif's number from one of the girls before I left.

Saturday, 7 November

AMOS HITS BACK!

This morning, I sneaked Mum's handbag into my room and made a call from her handphone. It was to Bif. I waited till he picked up the phone, then I breathed heavily, and barked, "WOOF, WOOF, WOOF, WOOF, WOOF!" It was so satisfying, getting it all off my chest at 2am.

The return call came. Bif was really patient. He waited till 5am.

The phone rang and rang. Mum woke up and answered her handphone. Well, she was really angry. I heard her yelling into the phone, "You PERVERT! If you dare to call this number again, I will call the POLICE to track you down!"

I tried my best not to laugh so loudly. But if I had pressed the pillow any harder into my face, I'd have died for sure. Aw, poor Bif.

Really, Amos, making use of me like that! The poor boy, being shouted at. Stop using me as your mouthpiece!

FIERCE and NEUROTIC. Just what Bif needed. And how did she find this? I hid it with my Chinese books!

Friday, 13 November

Did my 100m freestyle today and came in under 1 minute 50 seconds. My personal best!

All of us have been training hard the last few weeks since after our exams. We can all feel the school spirit, but for some of us, the focus is not winning, but getting a freebie. Coach has offered a free handphone to the person who can swim the fastest for his part of the relay team – Michael and Alvin are vying for that. Anthony's mum said she would buy him the latest PlayStation game if our team won the inter-school swimming competition. As for me? Well, I just want to win. To get back at Bif, and to make my family proud of me. But everyone is busy at home, Mum is pre-occupied with Everest and Dad is busy with work. I don't think they realise I have a big competition coming up.

Sunday, 15 November

FAMILY CRISIS

Ah Kong was taken ill! Last night Po-Po called to tell us that he had chest pains and was admitted to the hospital. We went to see him this afternoon. He looked pale, but was really happy to see us. I showed him my new handphone and he managed to scroll through pictures of WPI and Everest on it. I left my handphone with Ah Kong. He said he would try playing games on it.

Oh man... Ah Kong had a heart attack last night. He had an allergic reaction to one of the medicines and it triggered a seizure. The doctor said he has to remain in the In-ten-sive Care Unit for a while. We all ate in silence tonight. I'm not sure if I can sleep.

Wednesday, 18 November

CURSED SIGN

The Merlion was struck by lightning! This can't be good. I'm really not superstitious, but this is too much. First, Ah Kong gets a heart attack, and now the Merlion is struck!

Friday, 20 November

SHOW & TELL

Somaly shared her story with us during Show & Tell today. I didn't know she came from such a humble background. She was a slum child, an orphan who was adopted into a missionary home. She learnt to read and write, and did so well in her studies that a group of sponsors paid for her trip to study in Singapore. She said when she first came to Singapore, she had no friends. Then she met other Cambodians studying in Singapore and now they are taking care of one another. She said she's excited to be in the school swimming team and hopes she will make it to the Youth Olympic Games one day.

After swimming practice, Somaly found me at a corner of the pool. I was in no mood to train and did not give my best today. We had a long talk and she told me about her childhood dream of leaving Cambodia. I was fascinated with her story. She said she used to have a picture of the Statue of Liberty pasted on the wall beside her bed. Each night before she slept, she would read a book using candlelight. She told herself to pretend she was Liberty, reading from the book in her hand, with light from her torch.

I asked why she liked the picture of the Statue of Liberty. Her answer almost made me cry. She said, "I want to learn English to free myself from hunger. I want to leave my country for a better future."

I decided to do a couple of laps after that. Somehow, my worries didn't seem much compared to what Somaly has gone through.

Saturday, 21 November

GET WELL SOON, AH KONG!

11am

I drew Ah Kong a picture. I drew his face over the body of the Statue of Liberty. He laughed when I told him it was a symbol to free himself from the hospital. Well, he must be getting better!

8pm

Our final competition is in a few days' time. I'm so worried about Ah Kong. Can't imagine losing him. I love him so much. How am I going to train without him behind me? The 3As will have no focus in training!

Monday, 23 November

THE MERLION

Woke up early this morning. Last night I saw some Singaporeans being interviewed on TV about the Merlion. All of them asked for it to be repaired – for the hole at the back of its head which was struck by lightning to be fixed. One man even suggested that a lightning conductor should be installed on the Merlion! I think it's strange how a symbol created by a lion's head and a body of a fish has come to mean so much to people. It's like having something shared.

Mum said the Merlion offers emotional attachment. She found something interesting for me to read. It was a poem written by Edwin Thumboo, called "Ulysses by the Merlion", and this poem has even been inscribed on the monument. He called the Merlion a "lion of the sea."

In fact, Mum said many poets like to write about the Merlion! Poetry inspired by a national symbol. Hmmm... I like the term, "lion of the sea" and it is so apt for tomorrow's match. We are "lions of the sea" that will thrash Bif's team!

Wednesday, 25 November

THE FINAL SHOWDOWN

9am

This is it! This afternoon will determine if we are better than Bif's team. Our one chance of beating the arrogance out of him and his school.

7pm

Today must be the BIGGEST moment in my memory of swimming. The four boys got together to stretch and huddle, before getting into the pool. Then Somaly came yelling at me. She said Coach got a call from the hospital. Ah Kong's tests came back good, and he would be discharged. Somaly showed me Coach's handphone. It had a message, in full caps, "GO GET THEM, AMOS!" from Ah Kong – his first SMS ever, using my handphone. I dunked my head in the water when I started crying.

Then the most amazing thing happened. I saw Dad, Mum, Everest, WPI and Tom, making their way to the spectators'

stand. Tom was in a cat cage! And he had shocking pink goggles on his head! Oh man… my sister is still a nut case.

Immediately, I knew that our team would make it. With Ah Kong about to be discharged and Tom with his pink goggles, our swim team would win!

Michael was the first to swim, followed by Anthony. The two of them couldn't catch up with the leading team. When I went in third, we were a full body length behind the first team. From the corner of my eye, I saw Dad, Mum and my sister jumping and cheering. That seemed to give me more strength. I powered myself and cut through the water, gaining half a body length to close the distance. Alvin went in at the same time as Bif, the last swimmers for both teams. I think Bif's mistake was that he went out too fast, eager to beat Alvin. Alvin was cool – smooth, composed and swift.

At the turn, Bif was still half a body length ahead. With 20m to go, Alvin suddenly seemed to surge ahead. He swam close enough to ALMOST draw level with Bif. With 5m to go, both of them were level, and then Alvin touched HOME! We screamed our lungs out! Stomping our feet, we almost brought the roof down with our cheers! Alvin came in FIRST! Our HERO! We WON!!!

It was only when Alvin emerged from the water that we realised what a feat he had accomplished. His briefs were torn, and his underwear was showing! Alvin is the only boy I know who insists on wearing underwear beneath his briefs. It slows a swimmer down, but I guess his theory proved right today: "You never know when you might tear your swimming trunks. You wouldn't want everyone to see your backside, right?"

Someone stripped Alvin of his swimming briefs, exposing his polka-dotted underwear. His briefs were strung up on a pole, and Michael ran round the swimming pool, flying them high. This was the school's proudest moment – swimming history made for our first boys' relay team. I saw Michael going over to hug Alvin. Finally, he gets it. We are all part of the same team. I am really happy.

Thursday, 26 November

GETTING BACK TOGETHER

The four boys, with Somaly and Coach, got together to celebrate our victory. We had pizza at a restaurant. We were making such a ruckus that the restaurant manager came over to tell us to quieten down. He said there was an unhappy diner in the restaurant.

Halfway through our meal, I saw Bif come in with his Mum. Just at that moment, my handphone rang. I have a new ring tone, and it is really loud. It goes, "EEEEEEEIIAUUUWWW!" Bif turned, saw me and swore at me with a bad sign. His mum saw what he did and twisted his ear so hard that he shouted out. Good for her!

That should teach him some manners.

He was glaring at me as I barked into my phone, "WOOF, WOOF, WOOF!"

Bif's mum was really nice. She made Bif shake our hands before they left the restaurant. Although I could see he was reluctant.

I'm so proud of you, Amos! Congratulations on coming in 1st! And that's the right spirit of competition — having friendship and respect for one another!

Sunday, 29 November

A BETTER LIFE

Having seen Bif's mum, I'm convinced that she's no different from my mum. She can't stand her son to be disrespectful. And I'm sure like Mum, she worries about her son's grades in school. Somaly is worse off – she has no parents and she's on her own studying in Singapore. Yet she's serious in studies and sports.

What is it about both of them that drives them so hard? Maybe "Mum Power" for Bif, but I think it's just, HUNGER. Hunger to be better off in life. Coach had said that both Michael and Bif have in them the hunger to train for success in swimming. There you see, Michael is also from a humble family.

Guess whether we call it hunger, drive, the fire to kill or

any other name, it's the attitude that determines a winner. And it shouldn't be one where we look down on our opponents who have lost. Nor should we be arrogant about winning. Michael learnt something when we won. I hope Bif did too.

DAD'S OLYMPIC TALK

Dad spoke to me tonight. He told me about his childhood dream of wanting to be the fastest runner in the world. It was from watching all those TV programmes on Carl Lewis, Sebastian Coe and Steve Ovett. Dad said he was simply driven by heroes who were bent on winning, and he wanted to be like them. Having the Olympic dream drove his hunger in studies, sports, and now work. I guess it's the same with Michael. He finds time to juggle both studies and sports well, as he's hungry like how Dad was.

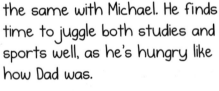

I'm probably more serious about swimming now than I was at the beginning of the year. But I have a long way to go, before I can cultivate the sort of hunger that Somaly, Michael or Bif have. But Dad's right, we need to dare to dream, to be like the best, to spur us on to do better, one step at a time.

ALL ABOUT HAPPY THINGS!

We are celebrating WPI's birthday next week. I am planning a party for her. Just for the family. I showed WPI what I got for her birthday. It was a yo-yo! Boy, she's really crazy about it. Everyone in school is playing with this. WPI did a "walk the dog" with her yo-yo, and Everest was gurgling and clapping in excitement. Really, they deserve each other! One's a dramatic performer, and the baby's too dumb to boo her.

I'm looking forward to the remaining weeks of the holidays. Dad said we will be going for a short holiday. I wonder where we are going?

MY LAST ENTRY

I told Mum I wouldn't be writing in my diary when we're on holiday. She said I could use Dad's laptop to start a blog online. Hmm... that's interesting.

Let's see, maybe my blog could look something like this:

Amos Lee
11 years of age
School Swimmer
Toilet Diarist

SOMETHING ABOUT ME...

I live in a flat and have a three-legged cat for a pet. An unlicensed one. I am Big Brother to a sister who is crazy about the yo-yo, and a six-month-old baby brother.
I wrote a Science magazine which

won an award. I am an expert on how babies are made, both spider and human ones.

I am loyal to my friends, Alvin, Anthony and oh alright, Somaly, Alvin's girlfriend too! I am good in swimming, but I can do better with further training. I have been swimming competitively for one year, and I have learnt the values of friendship and respect through my training in sports. I have also discovered something about hunger, not the sort where you want to eat food, but the sort that drives you to want to win in a competition. I feel strongly about building team spirit with my swim mates, and I hope to do my best in more swimming competitions. For a start, I would like to write a school cheer that can be used in the new semester.

Half-beast, Half-fish,
Lions of the Sea,
Masters of the Game,
UNITY IS KEY!
To-ge-ther, as ONE!

Right, someone is banging on the bathroom door. Got to go!

I look forward to posting my first blog online next year. I will only reveal my blogspot address to my best buddies. That's right, friends, and NOT my mum!

I can always google to find you, Amos darling!

A

Asian Youth Games	The first Asian Youth Games was held in July 2009 over nine days involving 1,300 athletes from 45 National Olympic Committees. Singapore won 30 of the 272 Asian Youth Games (AYG) medals, finishing with 9 golds, 6 silvers and 15 bronzes. Singapore finished third in terms of total medals behind South Korea and China.

C

C. Kunalan	C. Kunalan is Singapore Sportsman of the Year 1968-1969. Singapore's sprint champion in the 60s, his 100m record clocked in 1968 stood for 33 years before it was re-written in 2001. He is currently a lecturer at the Physical Education and Sports Science Academic Group, National Institute of Education.
Carl Lewis	Carl Lewis, born in 1961, was a dominant American sprinter and long jumper from 1981 to the early 1990s, winning 10 Olympic medals (9 golds) and 10 World

	Championships medals (8 golds). In 1999, he was voted "Sportsman of the Century" by the International Olympic Committee.
Cat Welfare Society	The Cat Welfare Society is a non-profit organisation run almost entirely by volunteers. The Society's mission is to save lives through sterilisation and bring down the community cat population through more effective and humane long-term methods.

Edwin Thumboo	Edwin Thumboo is an award-winning Singaporean poet and academic who is regarded as one of the pioneers of English literature in Singapore. He is often dubbed Singapore's unofficial poet laureate because of his poems with nationalistic themes, notably 9th of August — II (1977) and Ulysses by the Merlion (1979), which was published in the anthology of the same name. Ulysses, which references an iconic statue of a beast with the upper body of a lion and the tail of a fish called the Merlion that faces Marina Bay, was inspired by the use of Irish mythology and history by W. B. Yeats. Thumboo received Singapore's first Cultural Medallion for Literature in 1979.
Empire State	The Empire State building is the tallest building in New York, after the destruction of the World Trade Centre towers on 11 September 2001. Completed in 1931, the 102-storey Empire State Building is the third tallest skyscraper in America and the 15th tallest in the world.

Ian Thorpe	Ian James Thorpe, nicknamed "Torpedo" by the Australian media, is regarded as one of the greatest Australian middle-distance swimmers of all time. In his career, he won 5 Olympic gold medals, more than any other Australian. In 2000, he was named Young Australian of the Year. He announced his retirement from competitive swimming in 2006.

M

Merlion struck by lightning	On 1 March 2009, the Merlion was struck by lightning, which left a gaping hole at the rear of its head. It has since been repaired. The date used in the book is a fictitious one.
Michael Phelps	Michael Phelps swam in the 2000 Summer Olympics in Sydney as a 15 year old in a single event, the 200m Butterfly, finishing fifth. Since then, he has gone on to win 8 gold medals in the 2008 Beijing Olympics, surpassing the feat of Mark Spitz who won 7 gold medals at the 1972 Munich Olympic Games.
Mount Everest Women's Team from Singapore	The team of three Singaporean women, Lee Li Hui, Esther Tan and Jane Lee reached the summit of Mount Everest on 20 May 2009. A second team of two women, Lee Peh Gee, and Joanne Soo also reached the summit two days later on 22 May 2009. www.womenoneverest.com

S

SPCA	The Society for the Prevention of Cruelty to Animals is a registered animal welfare charity that aims to promote kindness and prevent cruelty to animals and birds. The SPCA in Singapore receives about 700 unwanted pets and stray animals every month.
Sebastian Coe	Sebastian Coe, born in 1956, was a middle distance runner from England. He won the 1,500m gold medal at the Olympic Games in 1980 and 1984. He was the first man to break the 1 minute 43 seconds, and 1 minute 42 seconds barriers in the 800m event. Lord Coe, as he is now known, is now the chairman of the London Organising Committee for the 2012 Olympic Games.
Steve Ovett	Stephen ("Steve") Ovett, born in 1955, was a middle distance runner from England and a gold medalist in the 800m at the 1980 Olympic Games. His rivalry with Sebastian Coe dominated sports headlines all over the world, inspiring legions of aspiring runners.

T

| Tao Li | Tao Li, a China-born Singaporean, is the first Singaporean to make an Olympic swimming final. At 19, she finished fifth in the 100m Butterfly Finals at the Beijing 2008 Olympics Games. She was Singapore's Sportswoman of the Year in 2007 and 2008. |

W

| We must, we must, we must increase our bust! | This is a line borrowed from Judy Blume's book, titled "Are You There God? It's Me Margaret" |

Y

| Youth Olympic Games | The inaugural Youth Olympic Games (YOG) will be held in Singapore from 14-26 August 2010. It is a 26-sport event, involving about 4,500 athletes and officials. It will be the debut of the International Olympic Committee's (IOC) new initiative to engage the world's youth. |

ABOUT THE AUTHOR

Adeline Foo is an MFA graduate of New York University's Tisch School of the Arts, Asia. She has 18 published children's books, with five national bestsellers. The Diary of Amos Lee: I Sit, I Write, I Flush! won the inaugural Red Dot award for 'Best Junior Fiction' presented by the International Schools Libraries Network of Singapore in 2009. The Diary of Amos Lee is also published by Hachette India and Lentera Hari in Indonesia. The books were adapted for a 10-part TV series for Singapore MediaCorp children' channel, okto, from 25 January to 28 March 2012.

ABOUT THE ILLUSTRATOR

Stephanie is a senior designer at Epigram, a local publishing house dedicated to producing exquisitely-designed and thought-provoking books (www.epigrambooks.sg). Illustrations for this book came about from observing scenes and people at work, cafes, libraries, East Coast park, and while cat-sitting Sev and Tig. For other adorkable (dorky and adorable) stuff that Stephanie has done, head to www.steffatplay.blogspot.com.